Where on Earth Did the Bible Come From?

Where on Earth Did the Bible Come From?

A Study of the Development of the Bible

WILLIAM MILLER FULKERSON

Foreword by Peter Rhea Jones

WIPF & STOCK · Eugene, Oregon

WHERE ON EARTH DID THE BIBLE COME FROM?
A Study of the Development of the Bible

Copyright © 2020 William Miller Fulkerson. All rights reserved. Except for brief quotations in critical publications or reviews, no part of this book may be reproduced in any manner without prior written permission from the publisher. Write: Permissions, Wipf and Stock Publishers, 199 W. 8th Ave., Suite 3, Eugene, OR 97401.

Wipf & Stock
An Imprint of Wipf and Stock Publishers
199 W. 8th Ave., Suite 3
Eugene, OR 97401

www.wipfandstock.com

PAPERBACK ISBN: 978-1-5326-7651-2
HARDCOVER ISBN: 978-1-5326-7652-9
EBOOK ISBN: 978-1-5326-7653-6

Manufactured in the U.S.A.   02/24/20

Contents

List of Illustrations and Charts	vii
Foreword by Peter Rhea Jones	ix
Preface	xi
Acknowledgements	xiii
Introduction	xv
Author Vitae	xvii
1 │ Why Study the Bible's Development?	1
Chapter 1 Study Guide	9
2 │ The Development of the Old Testament	11
Chapter 2 Study Guide	20
3 │ Writing a History of the Jewish People	22
Chapter 3 Study Guide	33
4 │ The Influence of David and Solomon	35
Chapter 4 Study Guide	43
5 │ The Development of the New Testament: The Gospels	45
Chapter 5 Study Guide	56
6 │ The Development of the New Testament: The Other Writings	59
Chapter 6 Study Guide	68
7 │ Putting it All Together	71
Chapter 7 Study Guide	78

8	Jerome and the Latin Vulgate	80
	Chapter 8 Study Guide	*87*
9	From Rome through Europe	89
	Chapter 9 Study Guide	*97*
10	Beginnings of the English Language	100
	Chapter 10 Study Guide	*108*
11	The Development of the English Language	109
	Chapter 11 Study Guide	*114*
12	William Tyndale, Miles Coverdale, and Others	116
	Chapter 12 Study Guide	*124*
13	The First Completed Printed English Bible	126
	Chapter 13 Study Guide	*133*
14	The King James Version of the Bible	135
	Chapter 14 Study Guide	*145*
Bibliography		149
Index		155

List of Illustrations and Charts

Ancient Manuscript Scroll
Navajo Storyteller
Sample of Cuneiform Writing
Moses
Front Cover of the Septuagint
Copy of Aleppo Old Testament
Fragment of Ancient Greek New Testament
Front Cover of an Ancient Copy of the Vulgate
Illustration of St. Jerome
Illustration of St. Anthony
Christian Monastic Missionary Movement
Illustration of St. Bede
Wycliffe's Lollards
Illustration of John Hus
Illustration of Tyndale
Illustration of Mark Coverdale
Burning Execution of Tyndale
John First Chapter Coverdale Bible
Original Copy of Coverdale Bible
Illustration of King James
Illustration of "The Learned Men"
Figure 1. A Probable Order of Old Testament Writings and Collections
Figure 2. An Approximate Chronology of New Testament Writings
Figure 3. History of the Expansion of Christianity in Europe

Foreword

Our author, long term in ministry, has stuck by the stuff. Bill has maintained consistently a commitment to Christian social ministry. From early on, he has brought along an academic bent as well. Of interest is that Dr. Fulkerson speaks Espanol, relevant to his mission.

Here in touch with his audience and with a notable passion to communicate he has produced a good textbook. He desires to inform and empower the laity in an area of biblical understanding belonging to theological education as a standard topic. He recognizes that the laity needs this missing piece in their own biblical education and would benefit significantly.

Dr. Fulkerson, in his carefully thought out outline and progression in this book, releases an orientation that will open up fresh insights of the kind that will leave a lasting impression. He has done his homework.

With this study you the student will be less dependent and more individually able to do interpretation.

Take and read.

DR. PETER RHEA JONES
Formerly professor at Southern Seminary and
McAfee School of Theology, Mercer University

Preface

This book began as a series of lectures given to members of the First Baptist Church of Decatur, Georgia. The course, "A Study of the Development of the Bible," was designed to inform the lay members of the church regarding the historical development of the writings that came to be called "the Bible."

There are many studies of particular books of the Bible. There is also a myriad of devotional and inspirational books regarding the Bible. However, the members of this class indicated that they had never studied how the Bible came to be written, although much of the contents of this series may be found in the prefaces and introductions of the various translations of the Bible in their possession. The author of this study believes that the Holy Spirit of the One Holy Creator oversaw the collection of materials, the writing, and eventually the selection of writings that make up the Bible. He also believes that this development was a natural process of people who worshipped *Yahweh,* or *Elohim,* or one of the many names given to the Hebrew's one God.

As you study this material, be sensitive to the fact that these materials that were collected over three thousand years could not just have happened. There was a divine oversight that permitted the natural means of assembling and producing this collection of writings.

Also, as you study this material may you come to appreciate and love even more deeply the Scriptures of the Jewish and Christian peoples, many of whom gave up their lives that we might have the Bible in our language today.

Acknowledgements

This writer is grateful for the First Baptist Church of Decatur, Georgia which for many decades has maintained a spirit of inquiry, of seeking the truth, of acting on its findings, and of encouraging the gifts of its members. It is a missional church that has, through many decades, spawned new congregations both in the United States and worldwide. It has resettled Cambodian refugees and started a Cambodian Church with them. These people came to America as Buddhists and animists and became strong Christians who return annually to Cambodia to witness to friends and families. The First Baptist Church was an early participant in the civil rights movement and encouraged women in all roles and positions of the church.

The writer is also indebted to the Southern Baptist Theological Seminary of Louisville, Kentucky and the professors of many years ago who suggested and led this writer to assemble a library of ageless and classic study books.

He appreciates the leadership of the interim pastor of his church, Dr. David Gushee, professor of Christian ethics at the McAfee School of Divinity of Mercer University. His development of a Wednesday evening series of serious studies, entitled "First Baptist University," enabled this writer to develop this book.

Without the sharp eyes of my wife, Carol Stuckey Fulkerson, who proofread and edited the manuscript, this book would contain many, many more errors than it currently does.

ACKNOWLEDGEMENTS

Lastly, to the many nameless followers of the One True God, who gathered from here and there, who remembered this story and that tale, who collected and assembled and memorized what eventually became the Scriptures of the Hebrews, and to the writers of the Gospels and other early Christian writings, then to such scholars as Jerome, Wycliffe, Tyndale, Rogers, and Coverdale who literally gave their lives so that English-speaking people might have the Bible in the English language, I am indebted.

All Scripture references, unless otherwise indicated, are from *The Revised Standard Version of The Holy Bible*, Copyright of the RSV, 1946, by the Division of Christian Education of the National Council of Churches of Christ in the United States of America.

Assistance in matters of copyright law was provided by Bobby Slotkin, attorney in Decatur, Georgia, specializing in copyright law.

The author also wishes to acknowledge the technical computer assistance provided by Daniel Solberg, of *dSol Productions*, without which most of the paper would be lost in the dark shadows of cyberspace. This man is a master of keyboards, both of computer and also of piano and organ.

In Nomine Patris et filii et Spiritus Sancti

Introduction

The Bible ranks as one of the most important writings in human history. It is a "best seller." It adorns the bookshelves or coffee tables of most households in the Western World. It is quoted in more literary works than any other source. Its contents are studied, analyzed, researched, and debated in universities, colleges, literary circles, and bar rooms more than any other writing.

Some intellectuals scoff at it. Others simply ignore it, having never read it, or if they did read some portion of it could never see it applying to their lives or values. Some Christians "swear by it." That is, they rise up in anger against anyone who questions or disputes its teachings, even to the extent of violence against such persons. Many times, such persons have never really read the Bible. There is the often-heard claim, "Well, I believe the Bible," from those who do not realize all that is in this book.

This author grew up in a religious tradition that places the Bible at the center of its faith. There are special Bible studies, Sunday schools weekly study portions of the Bible. There are devotional books, hymn books, poetry books, children's picture books, and many other ways of bringing the Bible into the minds and lives of the faithful.

Yet, as this author recently discovered that even the most faithful lay university professors and corporate executives—all of whom are devout students of the Bible and faithful church men and women, Bible scholars in their own right—have little or no idea of *how* the Bible came to be.

Introduction

We will examine some of the theories of "inspiration" in this book. I have heard it expressed on several occasions that, "God said it, men wrote it, and that settles it!" This simple explanation thus eliminates all query and interest in the development of the Bible. It also raises many questions about many incidents in the Bible and certain inconsistencies. This author hopes to unravel some of the reasons for such possible conflicts of information that exist in the holy writings. Did the Bible just appear? Did it drop out of heaven carried by angels? Is it a mysterious writing that contains secrets and hidden codes waiting to be discovered and give salvation to the enlightened ones? This was a belief held by many Christians in the earliest days. They were called "gnostic" and believed that by discovering these secrets one would be saved.

So many misunderstandings of the Bible might be corrected by knowing how this wondrous book came to be. This writer hopes that the following writings might open eyes and minds to the very human/divine way that this book that we call *our* Bible came to be. May this be an adventure that leads the reader to an even deeper love for this word that tells about the Word, who is Jesus.

WILLIAM MILLER FULKERSON
Stone Mountain, Georgia

Author Vitae

WILLIAM (BILL) MILLER FULKERSON

Born in East St. Louis, Illinois. Married to Carol Jean Stuckey of Dupo, Illinois

He has two sons, William Bruce and Brent Alan, both veterans of the Middle East wars.

EDUCATION, TRAINING, AND EXPERIENCE

Bachelor of Arts. Southern Illinois University, Carbondale, IL Major: Spanish, Minors: French, Sociology, and Psychology.

Master of Arts. Southern Illinois University. Major: Spanish, Romance Philology. Minor: Linguistic Anthropology.

Bachelor of Divinity. The Southern Baptist Theological Seminary, Louisville, Kentucky.

Doctor of Ministry. The Southern Baptist Theological Seminary, specializing in Social Work, *Licensed Social Worker*, Kentucky, License #699.

Studies at Kent School of Social Work, the University of Louisville. Coursework in Social Statistics and Social Work Administration.

Certification in Spanish to English Translation, Georgia State University, Atlanta, Georgia.

ADDITIONAL EXPERIENCE

Served as Pastor of Baptist churches in Illinois and Kentucky

Served as Pastor/Director of two inner-city mission centers in Louisville, Kentucky

Served as Home Mission Board, SBC *Field Missionary* as Language Director, Atlanta Baptist Association

Chairman, St. Clair County (Illinois) Council on Alcohol and Drugs

Distinguished Citizen Award from the City of Louisville for neighborhood improvement projects

Director of Social Services, the Salvation Army, Atlanta, Georgia

Chairman, Georgia Advisory Council on Refugee Resettlement

Chairman, Atlanta Council of International Organizations (ACIO)

Member, Atlanta Association of Interpreters and Translators (AAIT)

Executive Director, Cross Cultural Concepts, Inc. (a nonprofit organization)

Retired as *Director of the Department of Refugee and Immigration Ministrie*s, the Home

Mission Board, Southern Baptist Convention

CURRENT INVOLVEMENTS

In retirement he translates documents to assist persons with immigration processes. He serves as interpreter in immigration proceedings. He is currently involved in writing two books. He currently enjoys teaching the Bible in his church as well as singing in the choir and in the Decatur Civic Chorus.

1

Why Study the Bible's Development?

In many and various ways God spoke of old to our fathers by the prophets, but in these last days he has spoken to us by a Son, whom he appointed heir of all things, through whom also he created the world.

—Heb 1:1–2

How the Bible came down to us is a story of adventure and devotion. It is a story of toil and faith by those who, sometimes at great cost, passed down from generation to generation the message of salvation. The Bible did not just happen nor has it been preserved through the years by mere chance.[1]

WHY STUDY THE BIBLE?

We read the Bible as a comforting book, or as an inspirational book. We read it for direction or specific passages that we usually ignore or skip. Occasionally, while reading, we have a "humm" moment, or a moment of confusion when we read something else

---

1. Lightfoot, *How We Got*, 11.

that does not match up. Sometimes we have trouble justifying some action or order initiated by God himself. But rather than pursue the question or that moment of revelation we simply let it slide by us. Most laypeople, many ministers and elders, and many seminary graduates are not aware of the way our Bible has been formed and delivered to us.[2]

In these next few chapters we are going to *study* the Bible. How did it come to be? Was it simply the development of men's minds, or did God have some part in it?

THE BIBLE IN EVANGELICAL/ PROTESTANT IDENTITY

There are several identifying factors in being evangelical Christian. Writers differ in what is the most essential quality in so being; there are four factors that stand out.

- The priesthood of all believers
- Separation of religion and government
- Freedom of conscience
- The sole authority of the Bible in matters of faith and practice

While this author is Baptist, and most of the resources in this lesson reflect Baptist thought, the values indicated here are shared by most Protestants and definitely by most evangelical Christians.

The Priesthood of All Believers

> Eileen Campbell-Reed writes,
>
> What does it mean to be *evangelical*? In order to answer this question we could look to history, current events, and consider the defining characteristics of the rich traditions of *Protestants*. Yet, a question remains, "What is the central feature of what it means to be *Evangelical*

2. Smith, *Our Bible*, vii.

Protestant. This means believing and living with conviction in the idea of the priesthood of all believers. The priesthood of all believers is at the very heart of being Evangelical.[3]

In order to help us better understand the concept of the priesthood of all believers and its implication, we must explore Scripture and our history. Historically, Protestants have looked to Scripture as a primary source of authority—the final means of interpreting the words of Scripture is through the living Word, Jesus Christ (John 1:1–5).

The late Dr. William Hull, New Testament professor at Southern Baptist Theological Seminary in Louisville and also dean of the graduate school and provost of the seminary, wrote:

"The contention that divided (Baptists from the Anglicans and Congregationalists) the claim of the official church that its authorized pronouncements embodied the true interpretation of the Bible; thus, any deviation represented a false understanding of Scripture. After all, ecclesiastical tradition beginning with the Apostolic Fathers represented centuries of cumulative effort by the most learned minds of the church to distill and apply the teachings of Scripture. How could the spontaneous interpretation of rank amateurs who lacked both training and supervision possibly overturn the carefully controlled interpretation of experts?"[4]

Hull continues by adding,

> The freedom to interpret the Bible afresh is not viewed by Protestants as license to substitute private opinion for long-standing consensus. But they know that Jesus promised the Holy Spirit to guide his followers into fresh truth (John 16:13), a promise the *first* Christians claimed as they reinterpreted the Old Testament in ways that it had never been understood before.[5]

---

3. Campbell-Reed, *Being Baptist*, 6. This writer changed Baptist to Evangelical.

4. Hull, *Baptist Experience*, 15.

5. Hull, *Baptist Experience*, 15.

Separation of Religion and Government or Separation of Church and State

Charles DeWeese has served as the executive director of the Baptist History and Heritage Society since 1999. He writes that:

> The primary feature of the Baptist genius is a biblically based, centuries old, won't go away focus on religious freedom. Derived from God's creation of every person in his own image, this freedom asserts the right of every person to make personal judgments about faith./ It claims that government should have no role whatsoever in matters relating to liberty of conscience. Not even the church has a right to force faith into patterns of conformity and uniformity. Every Christian and non-Christian should be totally free to make personal decisions about spiritual matters.[6]

In like manner, Walter Shurden, Professor of Christianity and Chair of the Roberts Department of Christianity at Mercer University, writes:

> For *Evangelicals*[7] the Bible is and always has been the final authority. It is the final authority in moral responsibility, in theological beliefs, and in human relationships.[8] BIBLE FREEDOM is the historic Baptist affirmation that the Bible, under the Lordship of Christ, must be central in the life of the individual and the church and that Christians, with the best and most scholarly tools of inquiry, are both free and obligated to study and obey the Scripture.[9]

---

6. DeWeese, *Freedom*, 6–7.
7. The author here substitutes "evangelicals" for "Baptists."
8. Shurden, *Baptist Identity*, 4.
9. Shurden, *Baptist Identity*, 13.

FREEDOM OF RELIGION

Closely tied to the emphasis on the priesthood of all believers is the emphasis on freedom of religion. The idea of religious freedom is tied directly to the idea of free access to the Bible. For many centuries the Bible was a book forbidden to the common Christian. It was written only in Latin—to own a copy of it in the language of the people was a crime punishable by death. It was commonly chained to the pulpit of a church.[10] It was when the Bible became accessible to everyday people that the reformation gained strength. DeWeese writes that,

> Freedom of religion is the historic Baptist affirmation of freedom of religion—*of* religion, freedom *for* religion and freedom *from* religion, insisting that Caesar is not Christ and Christ is not Caesar. Freedom shines through *Protestant*[11] history like an everlasting light. The light of liberty switched on for *evangelicals* the day they entered human history. It energized *their* origins by providing enormous spiritual power. It has electrified *evangelical* development by guaranteeing that liberty emphases would forever characterize *evangelical* trailblazing.[12]

Protestants insist on freedom of access to the Bible and freedom in its interpretation precisely because the Bible is the only means of arriving at the mind of Christ. The Bible is open to all believers. Believers must be free to interpret the Bible. This carries with it the responsibility to study and seek to understand the Bible. This demands the best of biblical scholarship. When studied in the context of the church, individual misinterpretations may be corrected.

Freedom functions as the central integrating theme of *evangelical* history. Coercion in faith and practice, the antithesis of freedom, has no legitimate place in church history, contemporary events, or future plans.

---

10. Bruce, *English Bible*, 67.
11. Italics are mine, substituting "Protestant" or "evangelical" for Baptist.
12. DeWeese, *Freedom*, 9. Italics mine.

THE BIBLE IS THE SOLE AUTHORITY OF FAITH AND PRACTICE

William Hull writes of "The Sufficiency of Scripture":

> Baptists have long been known for their reliance on the Bible as "the sole rule of faith and order." In their early conflicts with the established church, this axiom championed the teachings of Scripture over every form of ecclesiastical tradition that regulated the content of faith, such as creeds and the rulings of councils. . . . Thus the "Bible only" battle cry of the Baptists and Lutherans was an audacious attempt to oppose both civil and ecclesiastical authority by appeal to divine authority . . . That is, to set God above both church and state.[13]

Just as evangelicals insist that the approach to God be direct and immediate, so must the access to Scripture be just as open and unencumbered without first filtering its truth through the lens of the reigning consensus. Only in this way does the unfettered Word retain its freedom to reform the church itself.

Walter Shurden concurs when he writes, "The Bible is final, but human understanding of the Bible is never final nor complete nor finished."[14] For evangelicals, the Bible is and always has been the final authority in moral responsibility, in theological beliefs, and in human relationships.

"Bible Freedom" is the historic Baptist affirmation that the Bible, under the lordship of Christ, must be central in the life of the individual and the church, and that Christians, with the best and most scholarly tools of inquiry, are both free and obligated to study and obey the Scriptures. There is a temptation today to hide behind doctrinal creeds, covenants, signatures, and ecclesiastical bodies.

Baptists and others have traditionally shied away from creeds. *First,* no doctrinal statement can adequately summarize the biblical mandate for behavior and belief. *Second,* creeds make

---

13. Hull, *Baptist Experience,* 15.
14. Hull, *Baptist Experience,* 16.

themselves the norm and then force compliance to it. Representative Brooks Hays (Dem. Arkansas), who was President of the Southern Baptist Convention 1958–1959, wrote, "I furthermore accept Baptist insistence that we should not have creeds. I have sometimes been amused to see ministers and even congregations vigorously oppose departure from a set of teachings—despite our firm non-creedal position . . . I could chuckle with a Presbyterian friend of mine who said 'The difference between you Baptists and us Presbyterians is that we have a creed that we don't live up to, and you don't have a creed, but you live down to one.'"[15]

CONCLUSION AND SUMMARY

To study the Bible correctly some questions must be asked and answered.

- What did the biblical statement mean in its original setting?
- Why was this particular section written?
- Under what circumstances was it written?
- What do we know of the writer?
- What do we know of the historical setting?
- Do we understand that the Bible was originally *written* in Hebrew, Aramaic, and Greek, but that the speakers *spoke* Aramaic and ancient Hebrew?

What About Me?

When I read the Bible do I:

- mainly seek comfort, guidance, or information?
- notice *new* insights or information? Do I make note of these?
- ever notice something that seems strange, out of place, or at odds with something somewhere else in the Bible?

15. Childers, *Way Home*, 162–63.

- ever stop and think or say, "humm"?
- ever stop and say, "aha"?
- seek *to get out* of the Bible more than *to put into* the Bible?
- realize what a *dangerous* and *revolutionary* book the Bible is? It is most feared and banned by those who fear the truth and who fear open enquiry and discussion. It helped to topple the Berlin Wall; it helped to unravel the Soviet Union. It has toppled dictators and emperors. It has outlasted those who have tried to silence or destroy its words.

Sir Walter Scott wrote these words about the Bible:16

> Within that awful volume lies the mystery of mysteries.
> Happiest they of human race to whom their God has given grace.
> To read, to fear, to hope, to pray, to lift the latch and force the way;
> And better had they ne'er been born
> who read to doubt, or read to scorn.

CHAPTER 1 STUDY GUIDE

Two new ways of studying the Bible might produce a response of: _____ or maybe _____.

Several factors in evangelical identity are:

1. _____
2. _____
3. _____
4. _____

Eileen Campbell identified the "central feature of being Baptist" as the _____ of all believers.

The priesthood of all believers means _____
_____
_____.

For evangelicals, the Bible is _____
_____
_____.

Why do Baptists not have a creed or creeds? _____
_____
_____.

The final authority for belief and practice of faith for Protestants is _____.

What are some questions to ask if we *seriously* study the Bible?

1. _____?
2. _____?
3. _____?
4. _____?

Why is the Bible such a feared and dangerous book? _____
_____
_____.

WHERE ON EARTH DID THE BIBLE COME FROM?

SUGGESTION: Read the *foreword or preface* of your Bible. Write down any of the new information you find.

2

The Development of the Old Testament

I hope all of us would agree that the Bible is not an ordinary book. There is something special about it. The word "inspired" means "breathed into." God's Spirit has breathed into the writing and development of the Bible. There are at least four theories regarding the inspiration of the Bible:[1]

- The dictation view
- The limited inspiration view
- The plenary verbal view
- The neo-orthodox view

THE PLENARY VERBAL INSPIRATION VIEW

The word "plenary" means *complete* or *full*. "Verbal" means "*the very words of Scripture.*" So, this view means that every single word of Scripture in the Bible is the very word of God. It's not the idea

---

1. See, "What Are the Different Theories."

of every thought that is inspired, but words themselves. Second Timothy 3:16–17 uses a unique Greek word, *theopnuestos*, which literally means "God breathes." Scripture is a breath out of the mouth of God.

Furthermore, *prophecy* never had its origin in the human will, but prophets, though human, spoke from God as they were carried along by the Holy Spirit. This is the traditional view of historical Christianity and is retained by most conservative churches today.

THE LIMITED INSPIRATION VIEW

The limited inspiration view says that God guided the human authors but allowed them freedom to express themselves in their works, even to the point of allowing factual and historical errors in the historical accounts. Fortunately, the Holy Spirit prevented any doctrinal errors.

This raised the problem that if the Holy Spirit allows errors in the historical accounts, how can we be sure he does not allow errors in the doctrinal accounts, since doctrine is woven into the historical accounts all the way through the Bible?

THE DICTATION VIEW

God is seen as author and the individual writers as secretaries taking dictation. God spoke and men wrote it down. The bottom line is that the dictation theory only explains certain portions of Scripture but not all of it, or even most of it.

THE NEO-ORTHODOX VIEW

The transcendence of God is emphasized, that God is so different from man that we could never know his thought through direct revelation. Furthermore, this view denies that the Bible is "*the* Word of God," rather that the Bible is a witness or mediator to the living Word of God, who is Jesus. The words in the Bible are not

God's words, but the words written by fallible men. The Bible is only inspired in that God can use the words to speak to humanity.

Somewhere in this mix we can form our own view. However, two passages help us to understand the mechanics of "inspiration" that gives credit to the conscious, intentional goal of the writers. Luke 1: 1–4, and John 20:30; 21:24–25—look them up!

BEFORE LANGUAGE WAS WRITTEN

For the Hebrews, the oral tradition was a way of recording their history and faith. it continued long after the Bible as we know it was written down. Nevertheless, that oral tradition lent itself to a great variety of forms. Genealogies served as historical records, proverbs provided memorable nuggets of instruction or codified acceptable behavior, and prophecies forecast the possibilities of dangers in the future. Poetry was common in all cultures with an oral tradition and rhythmic cadences of songs, psalms, hymns, and laments served as an aid to memory—both of the storyteller and his audience.

The 1908 discovery of a Neanderthal grave in La Chapelle au Saints, France testified to the care which Neanderthal man already lavished on his dead, but it was a token of something more. Had the dead been accorded such a secure, indestructible, and durable grave had there not existed a firm *conviction that there was a life after death*? Certainly, the idea that death may not be the end of all things seems to have been in evidence here. Man's conviction that there is a life after death expresses itself in the stones which he erected to protect his dead from the pressure of the surrounding earth seventy or eighty thousand years ago.[2]

Not only had Neanderthal man mastered the art of body painting, *but he probably believed in a single all-powerful god*. Once upon a time vital and remote, great and all-embracing, this single god seems to have degenerated in the course of hundreds of thousands of years. But certainly in the beginning he believed there

2. Lissner, *Man, God,* 181.

was *one* creator, not a polytheistic menagerie.[3] Although tales of the creation, of the flood, and of the patriarchs and their families started circulating as long ago as the events themselves, scribes probably did not begin to write down the lore of the Hebrews—the descendants of Abraham—until King David's reign in the tenth century BC. By then, many of the tales recorded were already centuries old, but they had been preserved and passed along through a much-respected tradition—*storytelling*. Storytelling was shared by peoples of the ancient Near East, as well as by scribes in Asia, Africa, and the Native Americans.

Ludwig Köhler writes, "There was an abundance of occasions for children to ask questions and seek information. Not every father will always have been able to satisfy them. But there were old men and women, wise, knowing elders, priests, storytellers and their words fell upon attentive ears. So from generation to generation the tradition and instruction were passed on in living form."[4]

The key to preserving all these tales was *the storyteller*. There were gifted individuals who performed that role for their community. The storyteller's job was more than simply entertainment. Their stories preserved the identity and collective memory of the people.[5] Hundreds of years after the scribes first began recording their stories, the spoken word remained a powerful force among Hebrews. Memory was still the storehouse of tradition and the oral tradition would continue side by side with the written, finding its most heartfelt expression in religious ritual. As long as memory preserved the faith, it would never be destroyed.[6]

THE BIRTH OF WRITING

Most of what is known about the laws and lifestyles of people from the times of the Old Testament comes from ancient texts—some

---

3. Lissner, *Man, God*, 182.
4. Köhler, *Hebrew Man*, 69.
5. Lissner, *Man, God*, 28.
6. Lissner, *Man, God*, 29.

The Development of the Old Testament

Figure of Navaho Storyteller. Photo by the author.

more than five thousand years old. The texts written, which appeared on clay tablets, stone monuments, statues, and even buildings, were inscribed in *cuneiform*, the earliest and once the most widespread form of writing in the Fertile Crescent.[7]

THE LANGUAGES OF THE OLD TESTAMENT

Little is known for certain about the *original language* of these desert tribes, whether the Hebrews had always spoken Hebrew, as the Bible leads us to believe, or if perhaps they spoke a dialect of Old Aramaic. By the sixth century BC the language of the Persian Empire, Aramaic (like Hebrew a Semitic language), had become the principal spoken language of the Near East.

The Israelite's medium of literature and sacred Scriptures continued to be in Hebrew. The Old Testament is written entirely

---

7. Friedman, *Who Wrote?*, 35

Example of Cunieform Writing.

in Hebrew with the exception of some chapters written in Aramaic and the occasional intrusion of a word or phrase written in another language. Aramaic appears in portions of Daniel (2:4—7:28) and Ezra (4:8–6, 18; 7:12–26); both passages refer to stories related to Persia. Some words and place-names in Jeremiah are in Aramaic. The Hebrew of some later books, Ezra, Nehemiah, 1 and 2 Chronicles, is heavily influenced by Aramaic vocabulary and structure. Also, Greek words appear in Daniel, and Persian words appear in Daniel and Esther. Remember that both Daniel and Esther are set in Persia.

THE PROBLEMS OF GENESIS 1-11

The name of Moses does not occur in the Hebrew text of Genesis. It was first used in the *Septuagint*, or the Greek translation (third

The Development of the Old Testament

Moses, the Law Giver.

or second centuries BC). There are some problems related to ascribing authorship of Genesis to Moses only.

There are the so-called "duplicate accounts," that is, more than one account of the same event. These accounts seem to come from several authors or tradition—the double account of creation (1:1—2:3; 2:4–25): twice, Abraham presents his wife as his sister (12:10–20; 20:1–18); three times he receives the promise of a son (15:4; 17:16; 18:10); more than once, Isaac's name is explained as "he laughs" (17:17–19; 18:12–13; 21:6); twice, Hagar is expelled from Abraham's household (16:4–14; 21:9–21); two accounts of God's instruction to Noah (6:19f; 7:2f); two accounts of sin entering into human experience (3:1–24; 6:1–8). This also raises questions about the "sons of God," the *Nephilim*, and the "giants," or men of renown. Certain statements indicate the writer was reflecting on a time long gone.

Joseph said he was "stolen out of the land of the Hebrews," but at that time it was known as the "land of Canaan" (40:15). Other references to the land of the Philistines: but they did not arrive until later (21:34; 26:1); Genesis 12:6 speaks of Canaanites *then* being in the land (12:6; 13:7); in 36:31 reference is made to the kings that reigned over Edom before there reigned a king over Israel—there were no kings of Israel until centuries later.

There were many types of tales told in the ancient Near East. Themes from Babylonian tales resurfaced in stories told by the Hittites and Canaanites, as well as by the Hebrews.

Creation stories and flood stories including a Babylonian tale called the *Epic of Gilgamesh* may be the basis for the Genesis story. Traces of an enormous flood dated at about 3500 BC. Note: Similar tales are found among the North American Native Americans and other cultures around the world.[8] These tales give credence to some enormous flood in early man's experience. Perhaps these are memories of the melting of the glaciers at the end of the Ice Age.

The people who lived nearly a hundred thousand years ago looked upon one god as the creator and sustainer of the world. Everything seems to indicate, as Genesis records and Saint Paul claims in his Epistle to the Romans (1:20), that man's knowledge of God dates from the creation itself.[9]

Abraham is the first Old Testament figure to be called a Hebrew. His descendants were commonly called after his grandson Jacob, or Israel, and thus bore the name of "the children of Israel" or "Israelites." The remaining chapters of Genesis trace the family of Abraham and his descendants until they become a tribe. The book ends with the story of Joseph and his importance in Egypt, thus setting the stage for the story of the exodus.

Man knows, believes, and lives by the fact that God loves us, because *something* happened in history to demonstrate his love.[10] Genesis must be approached with the belief that revelation means that God is disclosing of himself in mighty acts for salvation.[11] We may also realize that man's understanding of God develops, and he is completely revealed for our comprehension in Jesus Christ.

8. Huber, *Through the Ages*, 31.
9. Lissner, *Man, God*, 194. Noss, *Man's Religions*, 499.
10. Elliott, *Message*, 13.
11. Elliott, *Message*, 14.

The Development of the Old Testament

The Torah (the Law): The remainder of the books of the Torah are as follows:

- *Exodus*: This book tells the story of the expulsion of the Hebrews from Egypt and the role of Moses, the lawgiver and leader of the children of God.
- *Leviticus:* The book of the laws given by Moses to regulate the diet, social structure, behavior, and relationships of the people with each other and with God.
- *Numbers*: This is basically a population count of the Hebrew families.
- *Deuteronomy*: The "second law" that is a review of the history and laws contained in Exodus, Leviticus, and Numbers. Deuteronomy also contains the Farewell Address of Moses, as the people are on the verge of entering "the promised land."

CHAPTER 2 STUDY GUIDE

The Bible is an "inspired" book, not just like any other. What are four theories of "inspiration"?

1. _____
2. _____
3. _____
4. _____

Cite two passages of Scripture that indicate the conscious intention of the writers. _____

Before language was written, people recorded their history by means of _____ or _____.

Every community/tribe had history recorders called _____. Early Neanderthal and Cro-Magnon people believed _____ and _____ _____.

Most early cultures had stories about _____ and _____.

The earliest form of writing among cultures of the Near East was _____. Documents were written on _____ _____.

While the Hebrews wrote their literature and sacred writings in Hebrew, they spoke _____.

Some Old Testament passages were also written in _____ and _____.

What are some differences between the first and second creation stories? _____.

The book of Genesis ends with the story of _____.

The Development of the Old Testament

What are indications that parts of Genesis were written *after* the time of Moses?

1.
2.
3.
4.

_____ is the first Old Testament figure called a Hebrew.

Name the other four writings in the *Torah*

1.
2.
3.
4.

Leviticus means _____.

Deuteronomy means _____.

Revelation means _____.

How many books are in the Hebrew canon? _____

ASSIGNMENT: Study Genesis carefully to see if you can find anything that raises your eyebrows or causes you to say, "humm."

SUGGESTION: If you are *really* interested, read Leviticus to see what you can find that seems new, strange, harsh, or realistic.

3

Writing a History of the Jewish People

The story of the growth of Hebrew literature is in no fundamental way different from that of the growth of literature among other peoples. Everywhere, the beginning of national literature is *oral*. As people develop written language, they tend to put their stories and traditions and tales of heroes into written form. Among the Israelites we can recognize several types of forms of literature slowly developing into a fixed form. The Old Testament incorporates several types of literature:

- Fragments of an ancient song, "the Song of Deborah" (Judg 5)
- Archives and chronicles
- Laws
- Prophecies
- Worship books
- Proverbs and sayings

It is good to remember that the books of the Bible were not written in the order in which they appear in our Bible. Some of the writings are combinations or collections of various writings. Others may be only a portion of the original writing. *It is also important to remember that the writings of the Old Testament were the only Scriptures the early church had.*

No one knows how the books of the Hebrew Bible were chosen. The Bible itself says nothing about the considerations and concerns that led to selecting the canon, or authorized books. There are twenty-four books in the Hebrew canon, which is divided into three parts: Torah, Prophets, and Writings.

The Prophets have eight books: Joshua, Judges, Samuel, and Kings (known as the Former Prophets). and Isaiah, Jeremiah, Ezekiel and the Twelve (Latter Prophets) The Writings contain eleven books: Psalms, Proverbs, Job, Song of Solomon, Ruth, Lamentations, Ecclesiastes, Esther, Daniel, Ezra-Nehemiah, and Chronicles.[1]

The entire canon was completed sometime in the first century AD.[2] The five books of the Torah are believed to have been accepted as having spiritual authority during or just after the Babylonian exile in the sixth century BC.[3] Some of the literature is religious and some not.

"Two main questions should therefore be asked. How and why did the various books of the Old Testament come to be considered as having such religious authority as to be included in the canon of Scripture and why and how did other books come to be excluded?"[4] The Bible's sixty-six "books" were not all written at once, to make up the Bible, but at intervals through fully thousands of years, and in places all the way from Persia and Babylon to Rome.

JOSHUA

Deuteronomy ends with the death and burial of Moses, the great leader of this loosely affiliated group of tribes known as "Hebrews."

1. Jeffery, "Formation and Transmission," 33.
Huber, *Bible through the Ages*, 114.
2. Huber, *Bible through the Ages*, 115.
3. Huber, *Bible through the Ages*, 116.
4. Jeffery, "Formation and Transmission," 34.

They are poised on the frontier of their "promised land." As with European and American settlers in North America, the western lands they had their eyes on were already settled. Their promised land belonged to Philistines and Canaanites.

The book of Joshua tells of the battles fought to claim this land. A new period of great achievement opened for Israel when Joshua became their leader. The great task ahead of Joshua and the Israelites was to enter the promised land, conquer the inhabitants, and then hold possession of the land upon which they settled.[5] The leader of Israel was Joshua of the tribe of Ephraim, and the beloved lieutenant of Moses. He was an old, seasoned warrior of tested courage.

Israel's faith in God and his covenant with Israel gave them unfailing powers of endurance and kept their hopes of victory bright. They were not discouraged nor daunted by the many years required for them to conquer the nations opposing them.

During this era, the tribes were divided and given their parcels of land. Before his death, Joshua caused the people to assemble together in the city of Shechem and, like Moses, reviewed the solemn covenant between Israel and God.[6] Joshua, the servant of the Lord, died. They buried him in the border of his own inheritance in Timnath-serah.[7]

JUDGES

The death of Joshua left no one to take his place. Without a strong leader to hold them together, the tribes soon lost their feeling of being a united people, Israel (Judg 2:8-12). Each tribe, dwelling in its own land had to struggle alone against its hostile neighbors. It had little or no interest in the welfare of the other tribes.[8] The

---

5. Cohen, *Pathways*, 153.
6. Cohen, *Pathways*, 168.
7. Cohen, *Pathways*, 170.
8. Cohen, *Pathways*, 171.

judges were local Israelite warriors. In Canaan, the Israelites began to imitate the religious practices of the pagan people about them.[9] This remained the pattern of the Hebrews until the reign of David and into the reign of Solomon. But through Solomon's marriages to many non-Hebrew wives and consorts, the practices of worship of many other gods re-entered Israel and Judah.

In our study, we are not going to deal so much with the history and thought of the Hebrews and their faith. Our purpose is to understand *how* that faith developed through the growth of their Scriptures.

The mention of events in the conquest with Joshua and the subsequent settlement of their "promised land" is to show that there really are no consolidated people called the Hebrews, but rather a conglomerate of two loosely connected tribes. At this time there was no Scripture, no holy writings except for a code of laws assembled by Moses and the memory of the "covenant" between Abraham and God. This covenant would become the recurring tie that would bring the people back again and aim at the worship of the one true God, known by several names, but mostly as "I Am," or *Yahweh*.

THE FORMATION OF THE OLD TESTAMENT

The nineteen books of the Old Testament were written one-by-one to meet immediate needs. They were not all accorded the status of "Scripture," and some were only reluctantly accepted as such only after years of debate. They found their way up to that level gradually, after a historical development in which they proved their religious value. How and when did they begin to be so regarded? What were the stages of the extraordinary development that gave the Old Testament first to the Jewish people and then to the Christian Church?

In 2 Kings 22–23, we are told of the discovery in the temple of a religious law book, which became the law of the land through the energetic policy of King Joash. It is widely held that this book was

9. Cohen, *Pathways*, 172.

the code of law contained in Deuteronomy; if this view is correct, we have the first significant step in the establishment of the Torah as an authoritative religious document. The next comparable step in the development seems to have been the coming of Ezra to Jerusalem with a book of law which was accepted as normative by the Jewish community in and around the capital. Unfortunately, there is no universal agreement about neither Ezra's time of activity nor the identity of the law book. Most date this around the middle of the fifth century or beginning of the fourth century BC.[10]

THE CONTRIBUTION OF THE BABYLONIAN/PERSIAN CAPTIVITY

From 605 BC through the last eighteen years of its existence, Judah was a vassal of Babylonia. King Jehoiakim continued to rebel against Babylonia. However, he died before the Babylonian King Nebuchadnezzar could punish him. Finally, in 596 BC, Babylonia attacked Jerusalem, destroyed the temple, and burned Jerusalem and the surrounding towns to the ground. They took the holy vessels, including the Ark, to Babylonia.

The Babylonian captivity was of great significance in the development of Judaism and the Bible.[11] Without the temple, they could no longer worship as they had. During this time, they developed the synagogue.

Many biblical texts were collected and written down: the words of the prophets, the history books, such as Joshua, Judges, Samuel, and so forth. The Psalms were probably collected at this time. The Lamentations were probably compiled as a description of the destruction of Jerusalem.

When the Persians under Cyrus conquered the Babylonians, many of the Jews, including the elite and royal family, were taken to Persia. The religion of Persia was *Zoroastrianism*, the worship of *Zarathustra*. Here, the Jews were introduced to the concept of

---

10. Anderson, *Critical Introduction*, 15.
11. Huber, *Bible Through Ages*, 89.

Satan and the idea of spiritual conflict between good and evil. When the Jews were finally allowed to return to Jerusalem, these concepts were a part of their theology. "In the exile and beyond it, Judaism was born."[12]

THE FORMATION OF THE CANON

It has been argued that there was, in fact, no canon of Hebrew Scriptures until, at the end of the first Christian century, a synod of rabbis at Jamnia (or Yabneh), a few miles south of the modern Tel Aviv, defined its extent.[13] That the rabbis were disputing the exact limits of the canon during the Jamnia period is indispensable and understandable.[14]

The Hebrew canon was fluid, initially put in the form that we have today sometime around 350 BC. But it remained in various forms until somewhere around 300 AD. There was discussion among the rabbis about disputed books. Doubts existed about *Esther, Proverbs, Ecclesiastes, the Song of Songs,* and *Ezekiel*. The doubts centered about their use in public worship.[15] The writings that made up the Old Testament were not agreed upon until well after the time of Jesus. The Pharisees accepted as Scripture the books of Moses, the Prophets, and the Psalms. The Sadducees accepted only the books of Moses. Jesus quoted mostly from Deuteronomy, Psalms and Isaiah, aligning him more closely with the Pharisees.

THE FINAL SHAPE OF THE OLD TESTAMENT

As we shall see in a few weeks when we study the New Testament, the Hebrew Scriptures were still in an uncertain form. The Hebrew Scriptures, as Jesus knew them, consisted of twelve to twenty scrolls of different sizes. They were never united into what we would call

12. Bright, *History of Israel*, 323.
13. Anderson, *Critical Introduction*, 12
14. Anderson, *Critical Introduction*, 13.
15. Anderson, *Critical Introduction*, 17.

one book until the invention of the printing press made that possible in the fifteenth century AD. So, a "Bible" as we know it, even a Hebrew Bible containing the Old Testament by itself, was unknown.

In our Bible, the books of history begin with Samuel and continue through the kingdoms of David and Solomon up to the division into the two kingdoms of Northern Israel and Southern Judah. Many scholars now date the Chronicler's work about 300 BC on the basis of the genealogies in 1 Chronicles 3:17–24 and Nehemiah 10; 11; 12; 22.

The remarkable similarity in language between Chronicles and the memoirs of Ezra (7:27—9:15) suggests that Ezra was the Chronicler. Many old sources were employed, such as genealogies, court records of Israel and Judah, and writings of the prophets Samuel, Nathan, Gad, Ahijab, Shemaiah, Iddo, Jehu, and Isaiah.[16]

Part of the inheritance of Christianity from Judaism was Scripture. Jesus, in his preaching, constantly referred to this Scripture, and the disciples followed him in this practice.[17]

16. Lindsell, *Harper Study Bible*, 573.
17. Jeffery, "Formation and Transmission," 32.

THE GREEK *SEPTUAGINT*

Much of the development of the Old Testament into the form it now exists is tied closely to the international political events of the time following the Babylonian and Persian captivity. In simple form it goes like this: Babylonia captured Judah. Persia conquered Babylonia. Alexander the Great conquered Persia. He also conquered most of the Near East as far as India, and even Egypt. In so doing he spread the Greek language and culture throughout the region. The Roman Julius Caesar conquered the Greeks. So, the legal language of the area became Latin, but the literary language was Greek. Since so many of the Hellenistic Jews now spoke Greek, especially those living outside of Palestine, the rabbis began translating the Hebrew Bible into Greek.

This was called the Septuagint. Legend has it that the high priest in Jerusalem selected seventy-two scribes as translators of the Pentateuch (Torah, first five books of the Bible). The work was completed in seventy-two days with all seventy-two translators in agreement with the complete translation. In the Bible, in marginal notes, reference to the Septuagint is indicated by "LXX."

When Were the Bible Books Written?

There is little agreement among biblical scholars as to when or by whom most biblical writings came into existence. The more ancient the writings are, the more uncertain the origins. There *are* a few historical certainties. Kings David and Solomon are responsible for penning or collecting most of the wisdom literature that is the *Psalms, Proverbs, Ecclesiastes, the Song of Songs (The Song of Solomon)*. Also during the reign of David, much of the history, and possibly much of the traditions (such *as Joshua, Judges, Ruth*), might have been assembled. After Solomon and the division of the kingdom into the two kingdoms of Northern Israel and Southern Judah, most of the Minor Prophets ministered. During the Babylonian-Persian captivity the literature relating to that era came into being: *Daniel, Ezekiel, Esther*, most of *Isaiah*, parts of

*Jeremia*h. After the return from the exile and the re-establishment of the nation, the latter part of *Isaiah*, the *books of the Kings*, and other of the latter prophets were collected and written.

During the occupations of the Persians, the Greeks, the Seleucids, and finally the Romans, possibly *Esther, Nehemiah,* and the last prophet, *Malachi,* were written. It was also during this time that the books of *the Apocrypha* were written. An approximate chronological listing of the writings in what we call the *Old Testament* would be somewhat as follows:

Fig. 1: Possible Chronology of the Writing and Collection of Old Testament Writings

Job	Unknown. Many ancient Near East cultures had similar stories.
The Pentateuch (Genesis, Exodus, Leviticus, Numbers, and Deuteronomy, 1445–1405 BC)	Although written early, these were not given "Scripture" status until the Babylonian captivity.
Psalms, 1419–1450 BC	Written by David and others.
Joshua, 2050–1385 BC	
Judges, 1043 BC	
Ruth, 1030–1010 BC	A story of peace and love during the time of the Judges.
Song of Solomon, 971–965 BC	Written by Solomon, most likely.
Proverbs, 971–686 BC	Written or collected by Solomon.
Ecclesiastes, 940–931 BC	Attributed to Solomon.
First and 2 Samuel, 931–722 BC	Between 700–570 BC. The Hebrew elite were in Babylon and Persia.
Obadiah, 850–840 BC	
Joel, 835–796 BC	
Jonah, 775 BC	Most likely a parable to show God's favor on people other than the Hebrews.
Amos, 750 BC	
Hosea, 750–710 BC	
Micah, 735–710 BC	

Isaiah, 700–681 BC	Witten in Jerusalem, Babylonia, and Persia. Chapters forty-plus were probably written after the return to Jerusalem.
Nahum, 650 BC	
Zephaniah, 635–625 BC	
Habakkuk, 615–605 BC	
Ezekiel, 590–570 BC	The setting is in Babylonia but was probably written or collected later.
Jeremiah, 586–570 BC	Probably a collection of his sermons and actions by his secretary Baruch.
Lamentations, 586 BC	Biographical notes on Jeremiah written by Baruch.
First and 2 Kings, 561–538 BC	The history of David, Solomon, and later kings.
Daniel, 536–530 BC	The setting is in Persia.
Haggai, 520 BC	
Zechariah, 480–470 BC	
Ezra, 457–444 BC	
First and 2 Chronicles, 450–430 BC	Most likely written by Ezra.
Esther, 450–431 BC	The setting was Persia; this is the story associated with the holiday of Purim.
Malachi, 433–424 BC	
Nehemiah, 424–400 BC	The last prophet before John the Baptist.

Where on Earth Did the Bible Come From?

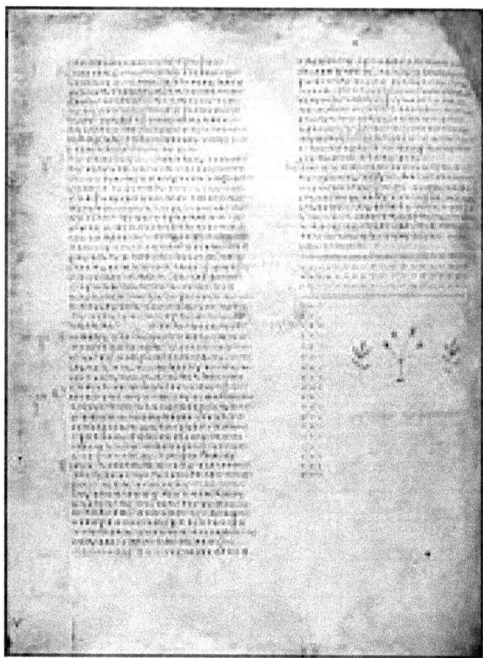

Fragment of The Old Testament from the Aleppo Codex, written around 930 AD in Tiberias. It is the oldest extant copy of the Old Testament, save for the documents found at Qumran near the Dead Sea.

CHAPTER 3 STUDY GUIDE

The beginning of a people's literature is _____.

Name some of the sources for the Old Testament writings:
_____
_____

What Scriptures did the early Christians have?
_____ _____

How were the books of the OT chosen? _____

When did the Torah begin to have spiritual authority? _____

What does "canon" mean? _____.

Deuteronomy ends with the death of _____.

The book of Joshua tells of_____.

What one item kept the Israelites together? _____

Who took Joshua's place when he died? _____

Who were the Judges? _____

Without going into the book of Judges, can you name any of them? _____

What are the final words of the book of Judges? _____
_____.

In _____ we are told of the discovery of a religious law book.

King _____ greatly enforced the laws of this book.

What two empires held the Hebrews captive? _____
and _____

Name several developments in the Bible that occurred in Babylon.

1.
2.
3.

Where on Earth Did the Bible Come From?

How did the religion of the Persians influence Judaism?

1.
2.
3.

What changes occurred in Judaism during the Babylonian captivity?

1.
2.
3.
4.

When were the Hebrew Scriptures finally set in the form we have today? _____

Name some of the books that had a difficult time being included:

1.
2.
3.
4.

The books of history begin with _____ and continue to _____

What is the Septuagint? _____

The legal language of the region in the time of Jesus was _____, but the literary language was _____.

How many scribes translated the Hebrew into Greek? _____

How would *you* describe the haphazard development of the Old Testament from such a variety of sources and circumstances?

ASSIGNMENT: In reading one or more of the Prophets, distinguish between "foretelling" and "forth telling." Compare the prophecies of Amos with Ezekiel. Good luck!

4

The Influence of David and Solomon

The Hebrew Scripture is divided into three sections: the *Torah* (Law or Pentateuch), the Prophets (*Nᵉbî'îm*), and the Writings (*Ketuvim*). The first five books, Genesis through Deuteronomy, traditionally ascribed to Moses, and the Law form the basic authoritative documents of Judaism. There follow twelve narrative works (*Joshua–Esther*) grouped together as *history*, five *poetical* books (*Job–Song* of *Songs*), and seventeen books of *prophecy* (*Isaiah–Malachi*).[1] For Orthodox Judaism only the first five books are authoritative. The Prophets are divided into two sections: Former Prophets (*Joshua, Judges, Samuel-Kings*; *Samuel-Kings* are considered one book) and the Latter Prophets (*Isaiah, Jeremiah, Ezekiel, and the Twelve; the Twelve* are *Hosea, Joel, Amos, Jonah, Obadiah, Micah, Nahum, Habakkuk, Zephaniah, Haggai, Zechariah,* and *Malachi*.) It is significant that *Lamentations* and *Daniel* are not included. The twelve Minor Prophets are counted as one, as they all fit on one scroll.

There is a third group which is a miscellaneous assortment of writings: the *Psalms, Proverbs,* and *Job*. These are known as the *poetical books*. There remain five short books known as the *Five Scrolls*. These are *Ruth, the Song of Songs, Ecclesiastes, Lamentations,*

1. Anderson, *Critical Introduction*, 10.

35

and *Esther*. For many centuries these books have been associated with specific festivals.

- *The Song of Songs* with Passover
- *Ruth* with the Feast of Weeks
- *Lamentations* with the Ninth of Ab (which denotes the destruction of Jerusalem)
- *Ecclesiastes* with the Feast of Tabernacles
- *Esther* with Purim

THE PROPHETS

We have already touched on *Joshua*. The *book of Joshua* is a sequel to the end of Deuteronomy and carries the story forward from the death of Moses to the death of Joshua. The contents fall into three parts: (a) chapters 1–7, the Conquest of Canaan; chapters 8–22, the partition of Canaan among the twelve tribes; chapters 23–24, Joshua's last words and death.

In the *book of Judges* are some stories of the conquest of parts of Canaan, stories of twelve national heroes who "judged" Israel. They are usually described as "major" and "minor." The basic theme of the *book of Judges* is: the people fall away from Yahweh; they are defeated by their neighbors in a series of battles; a judge arises to deliver them; they repent and turn again to Yahweh; and the cycle starts all over again. But the Prophets really begin with Samuel. He was the last of the *judges* and the first of the prophets.

WHAT CONSTITUTES ONE AS A "PROPHET"?

"The ancient Hebrews were never anything but a tiny folk occupying a mere crumb of a homeland, but they did produce those extraordinary characters called the "prophets"; it was this above all that made them so great. In the beginning, these prophets were in nowise unique. They were probably no more than witchdoctors and medicine men as in all primitive races.[2] By the eighth century, however, their character had completely changed. They had become men who by their moral courage rather than their magical powers preached ideals and morality instead of casting spells. They ceased to be primarily *foretellers* and became *forth tellers*.[3]

The prophet is one who speaks forth, speaks publicly, speaks out the word he has to speak. When he predicts, he speaks forth the future truth that would otherwise remain in concealment. When he speaks for another, he speaks forth the message which the other has committed to him, and which would otherwise have remained unknown. The thing uttered is often a divinely given prediction, but the word "prophecy" does not signify "to predict."[4] There are several words used in Hebrew in the Old Testament for "prophet." *Nabhi* is usually translated as "prophet." Except in five verses no other word is so translated. *Nabhi* and its forms are used several hundred times.[5]

In our English versions two different Hebrew words are translated "seer." Of the two, the one most properly used is *hozeh*. In the Aramaic it usually means "physical seeing." But in Hebrew it is mainly used to express "thoughtful insight or in connection with prophetic matters. David's friend Gad is described as a "seer" (2 Sam 24:11; four times in 2 Chron). The verb form is used in Isaiah 1:1—the vision of Isaiah, the son of Amoz.

The other noun translated "seer" is *roeh*. This is usually used for "*physica*l seeing." The English version makes no difference in translation between the two words. It is sometimes translated "behold" in the sense of seeing something important or divine.

It is in the account of Samuel's choice of Saul to be king over Israel that the prophets as a group make their earliest appearance in the Old Testament. They used music to induce a spirit of ecstasy and excitement. This so influenced Saul that he joined in with them in their prophesying. (1 Sam 10:10)[6]

2. Browne, *Wisdom of Israel*, 20.
3. Browne, *Wisdom of Israel*.
4. Beecher, *Prophets and Promise*, 21.
5. Beecher, *Prophets and Promise*, 22.
6. Fosbroke, "Prophetic Literature," 202.

WHAT DO WE MEAN BY "PROPHECY"?

We need to reiterate that the prophet is not necessarily a person who foretells, but one who speaks forth a message from the Deity.48 "Prophecy is not prediction, but it does not follow that prophecy does not include prediction. Beecher writes that "a prophet is a person who speaks publically." *Out of a special message that God has given him.*

For example: *Ezekiel, Daniel*, the first part of *Isaiah* are what we call "apocalyptic," as is the *book of Revelation*, and focused on future events. On the other hand, *Amos, Hosea, Malachi*, and these Latter Prophets are telling of God's displeasure with the moral and social abuses of the current day.

Amos proclaimed:

> Hear this, you who trample upon the needy, and bring the poor of the land to an end, saying "When will the new moon be over? That we may sell grain? And the Sabbath, that we may offer wheat for sale? That we may make the epah small and the sheckel great and deal deceitfully with false balances, that we may buy the poor for silver and the needy for a pair of sandals, and sell the refuse of the wheat?" (Amos 8:4–6)

Likewise, Micah prophecies future doom and punishment on both Israel and Judah because of their sinful practices. In this he addresses the moral and social ills of his day.

> Woe to those who devise wickedness and work evil on their beds! When morning dawns they perform it, because it is in the power of their hand. They covet fields, and seize them and houses, and take them away; they oppress a man and his house, a man and his inheritance. (Micah 2:1)

> Likewise, Micah prophesies future doom and punishment on both Israel and Judah because of their sinful practices. In this he addresses the moral and social ills of his day. Woe to those who devise wickedness and work evil upon their beds! When the morning dawns they

perform it, because it is in the power of their hand. They covet fields, and seize them and houses, and take them away; they oppress a man and his house, a man and his inheritance. (Micah 2:12)[7]

The pattern of the prophecies is this: because of the sin and evil of the people, God is going to send judgment on them, not on future generations, but on those who are currently disobeying the LORD. To these prophets it was thus given to discern in the actual course of events the supreme truth of the absolute righteousness of God. The prophets speak because they know that doom is inevitable.[8]

Most of the misunderstanding of prophecy is through trying to determine the end of the world through the apocalyptic works of prophets such as *Ezekiel* and *Daniel*. With close examination, these were observing the political situation of their day and pronouncing how it was going to affect Israel and Judah (or the Israel of the fourth and third centuries before Christ).

Refer to the timeline from the last chapter when the prophets were active (see Fig. 1). Many were active at the same time, some in northern Israel and others in the southern kingdom of Judah. A few, such as Micah, were active in both kingdoms. Malachi and Nehemiah were the last prophets, active some four hundred years before Christ, until John the Baptist. It was their ministry that enabled Israel's life as a people to survive the catastrophic end of its career as a nation and thus be the vehicle of God's continued revelation of himself.[9]

DAVID, SOLOMON, AND THE "WRITINGS"

David's sensitivity to poetry and music underlay most of his life, from the youthful shepherd to the king of a nation. This is evidenced in the number of psalms that are attributed to him. Some

---

7. Beecher, *Prophets and Promise*, 88–89.
8. Fosbroke, "Prophetic Literature," 207.
9. Fosbroke, "Prophetic Literature," 210.

of these psalms are set in the worship of Yahweh, but many are the expressions of his own joy, wondermment, anguish, and fear.

> O Lord, how many are my foes!
> Many are rising against me;
> many are saying of me
> there is no help for him in God. (Ps 4:1–2)

A recurring theme that runs through many of the psalms is this cry of frustration:

> I waited patiently for the LORD;
> He inclined to me and heard my cry.
> He drew me up from the desolate pit,
> out of the miry bog,
> and set my feet upon a rock,
> making my steps secure.
> He put a new song in my mouth,
> a song of praise to our God. (Ps 40:1–3)

This same cry for help recurs more than eight times. Yet we are all comforted with the words of assurance and praise that come from the Twenty-Third Psalm, "the LORD is my shepherd." The Psalms contain songs, prayers, complaints, faith, and assurance.

The present name for this book comes from the Latin *Vulgate*. Authorship includes David, Solomon, Moses, Asaph, and others. The final editing probably occurred during the time of Ezra. The individual psalms were written over many centuries. The Psalter was closely related to the Pentateuch (the five books attributed to Moses).

THE PLACE OF THE WRITINGS IN SCRIPTURE

The wisdom literature in the Old Testament includes Proverbs, Job, and Ecclesiastes. The sages whose role may have evolved from that of court scribe in King David's time are believed to have been responsible for an important body of Old Testament writing known as

THE INFLUENCE OF DAVID AND SOLOMON

"wisdom literature," including the books of Proverbs, Ecclesiastes, and Job. These sages were the rational men of learning who "gave counsel." They taught in the marketplace or by the city gates and instructed the people using proverbs, poetry, and stories.[10] King Solomon's traditional association with this material as the author of Proverbs and Ecclesiastes is probably due to his legendary judgment and skill at solving problems, his prayer for wisdom (1 Kgs 3:6–9), and the claim in Ecclesiastes that the author is a son of David.[11] While ascribed to very ancient authors, the three books are most likely of late origin. In their present form they belong to the period following 332 BC, the year Alexander the Great overran Palestine.

Many of the Proverbs in the Bible probably existed long before they were written down. Their poetic style makes them easy to remember. They were mainly riddles and rhythmic couplets used to teach virtues of common sense and ethical behavior.[12]

The book of Job may have its roots in a Sumerian tale called "Man and his God," which dates from around 2000 BC. It is likely that there was an ancient Hebrew tale that was recited orally, long before it was written down. Ezekiel refers to Job at the beginning of the Babylonian exile (Ezek 14:14, 20). Many scholars believe that the bulk of Job was composed during the Babylonian captivity. There may have been some portions added as late as 200 BC.

The book of Ecclesiastes is a more philosophical writing. It is a search for life's meaning as the author tries various paths trying to find meaning and happiness, with the conclusion that "vanity of vanities, all is vanity." Yet, the writer maintains that in "remembering his creator in the days of his youth" is the only way to meaning in life.

THE FIVE SCROLLS

The five short books, *Ruth, the Song of Songs, Ecclesiastes, Lamentations,* and *Esther,* are known as the "Five Scrolls" and are usually

---

10. Browne, *Wisdom of Israel,* 39.
11. Huber, *Bible through the Ages,* 66.
12. Huber, *Bible through the Ages,* 66.

associated with Jewish holidays. These books were included in the canon, not on their own merit, but because of association with Old Testament prophets or certain holidays (see above).

Ruth, a woman of Moab, was included primarily due to her familial tie to David. Ruth's husband, Boaz, was an ancestor of David. *Ecclesiastes* and the *Song of Songs* were included because of their association with Solomon. *Lamentations,* because of its ties to Jeremiah. *Esther* was the source of the holiday, *Purim.*

The Hebrew Scriptures (our Old Testament) were accepted as they now are by the third century BC. They were at that time translated into Greek as the *Septuagint* and accepted by the Christian Church by 50 AD. Jesus refers to them as Scripture. The apostles use them as authoritative in their writings.

In summary, we can repeat what the writer of Hebrews said in introducing his writing: "In many and various ways God spoke of old to our fathers by the prophets, but in these last days he has spoken to us by a son" (Heb 1:1).

CHAPTER 4 STUDY GUIDE

Name the three divisions of Hebrew Scripture:

1. _____
2. _____
3. _____

Name the four Latter Prophets:

1. _____
2. _____
3. _____
4. _____

The remaining books are called the _____.

These holidays are associated with what books?
    Passover _____
    Feast of Weeks _____
    Ninth of AB _____
    Purim _____

In the beginning, prophets were no more than _____.
    By the eighth century BC the prophets had become _____ instead of _____.

A prophet is a person who_____.

The pattern of prophecy is this: because of the _____ and _____ of the people, God is going to _____ on them, not on _____ generations, but on those who are _____ disobeying the LORD.

A great misunderstanding of prophecy is from people who are _____.

While most of the Psalms are related to David, others also contributed to writing Psalms. These were:
    _____, _____, and _____.

A recurring theme running through the Psalms is _____.

Other than the Twenty-Third Psalm, can you think of any other? _____

The wisdom literature includes _____, _____, and _____.

Solomon's connection to the wisdom literature is _____ and _____.

The conclusion of the writer of Ecclesiastes is _____.

His advice to young people is _____.

The "Five Scrolls" contain the short books of:
_____, _____, _____, _____, and _____.

The book of Ruth, a Moabite woman, is included because of ____ _____.

The book of Lamentations is ascribed to _____.
About 300 BC, the Hebrew Scriptures were translated into _____. This was called the _____.

In summary, we can understand what the writer of Hebrews said that _____.

ASSIGNMENT: Read Luke 1:1–4 and John 20:30; 21:24–25.

5

The Development of the New Testament: The Gospels

For eighty years, the Jews were independent of foreign control under the Hasmoneans until 67 BC when Queen Salome Alexandra died. She had left the kingship to her eldest son, Hycanus, but his brother Aristobulus also wanted the throne. He was commander of the army. Both men appealed to the Roman commander Pompey, who sided with Hycanus. In the summer of 63 BC Hycanus defeated his brother in a battle. But Roman intervention came at a high price: the Jews were forced to turn over their territorial possessions to the empire and submit to the Roman governor of Syria.

In 40 BC Parthian invaders overran the region. Herod, a military leader of Idumean origin and the son of a governor of Judea, fled to Rome where Mark Anthony and Octavian (later Caesar Augustus) persuaded the Senate to appoint Herod king of the Jews in absentia. The Romans swiftly defeated the Parthians, and in 37 BC Herod won Judea back.

During the years of Herod's reign, he expanded the boundaries of his kingdom nearly as far as King David's. On the site of the Second Temple he erected the largest and most beautiful place of worship the Jews had ever known. But many of the people hated Herod, a foreigner, whose claim to Jewish allegiance was through his Hasmonean wife. More distressing, Herod was a loyal friend of Rome.

Let's stop and define some terms. *Hasmoneans* ruled Judea from 116–63 BC. They were a result of the Seleucid (Alexander's) Empire but became independent in 116. They ruled through the high priest who also served as judge or political ruler. They were defeated by the Romans in 63 BC. Herod claimed title to the Jewish throne by virtue of a Rome appointment based on his marriage to a Hasmonean princess.

Parthians were a major force in Assyria (Iraq) and Persia (Iran) from 247 BC to 224 AD. *Seleucids* inherited the region from Babylon to Egypt from Alexander the Great. The *Seleucids* were a major force in hellenizing the region, especially Judea, and attempted to abolish Judaism and all signs of its worship. They were eventually challenged by the Maccabean rebellion and eventually over thrown by Rome.[1]

As king of the Jews, Herod assumed absolute control and killed off possible rivals among descendants of the royal dynasty. He also executed Hasmonean supporters in the seventy-member Jewish legislature known as the *Sanhedrin*. The gospel indicates that his bloody deeds culminated in the slaughter of the innocents, the infants in and around Bethlehem.[2]

When Herod died in 4 BC, Emperor Augustus divided the territory between Herod's three sons. Herod Archelaus was awarded the territory of Judea, which included Jerusalem. His brother Herod Antipas was given the territory of Galilee.[3]

Herod Archelaus was as ruthless as his father, but he lacked the political savvy of his father and lasted only ten years. His territory was turned over to Quirinius, the governor of Syria, who immediately ordered a census to evaluate the area's tax potential and the Jews would pay their taxes directly to Rome. The Jews thought this violated their obedience to God's Law. There followed

---

1. See "Hasmonean Dynasty"; "Seleucid Empire"; "Parthian Empire."
2. Huber, *Bible through the Ages*, 134.
3. Huber, *Bible through the Ages*, 134.

THE DEVELOPMENT OF THE NEW TESTAMENT: THE GOSPELS

a series of seven Roman governors appointed by Caesar. The most infamous of these was Pontius Pilate who ruled 26 to 36 AD.[4]

FROM MEMORIES AND STORIES TO COLLECTIONS OF WRITINGS

See: Luke 1:1–4, 2:17–19; Mark 14:51; John 20:30, 21:24–25

The early Christians had no printed books but used handwritten copies of the Christian writings. The early Christians' use of handwritten books is reflected even today in variations in the content of the various printings of the New Testament.[5] The original documents are all gone, without a trace. Many of the books were probably written on papyrus, which is no more durable than modern paper.[6] But before the originals were worn out and discarded, they were copied, some of them many times. They were meant to be read at group meetings and not to be stored away. Many hands touched them until they began to show wear and tear.

"Moreover the Acts of all the Apostles are included in one book. Luke addressed them to the most excellent Theophilus, because the several events took place where he was present; and he makes this plain by the omission of the passion of Peter and of the journey of Paul when he left Rome for Spain."[7]

Fig 2: An Approximate Chronological Order of the New Testament Writings

The Writing	Approximate year	Commentary
James	47–54, 51–69 AD	Disputed dates
1 Thessalonians	50, 51 AD	The first writing
2 Thessalonians	51 AD	From Corinth
Galatians	52 AD	From Corinth

---

4. Huber, *Bible through the Ages*, 136.
5. Colwell, "Text," 72.
6. Huber, *Bible through the Ages*, 40–41.
7. Bettenson, *Documents of Christian*, 39.

1 Corinthians	55, 56 AD	From Macedonia
2 Corinthians	56 AD	From Macedonia
Romans	56, 57 AD	From Corinth
Philippians	59, 61 AD	
Gospel of Mark	58–64 AD	First Gospel
Philemon	59–61 AD	
Colossians	60, 61 AD	61 AD Paul is imprisoned in Rome
Ephesians	60–62 AD	
1 Timothy	62–64 AD	Paul released
Titus	61, 63–65 AD	
2 Timothy	65, 65 AD	
Titus	61–66 AD	
Gospel of Matthew	62–69 AD	
1 Peter	63–65 AD	From Rome
Gospel of Luke	61, 64–68 AD	Paul is martyred
Hebrews	64–70 AD	
Acts of the Apostles	66–68 AD	
2 Peter	67–69 AD	
Jude	68–70 AD	Temple is destroyed
John's Gospel	83–90 AD	John banished to Patmos
1 John	85–95 AD	
2 John	86–93 AD	
3 John	86–93 AD	
The Revelation	94–96 AD	

The Development of the New Testament: The Gospels

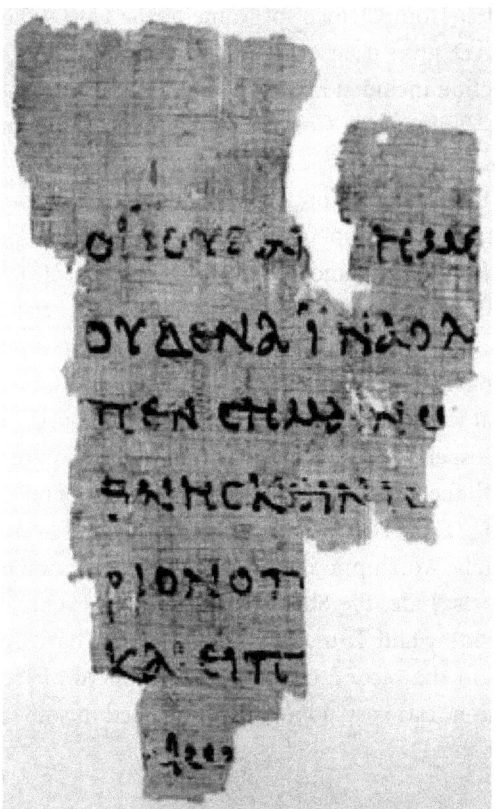

The books of the New Testament were not recognized as Scripture from the moment of their origin but came only gradually to such recognition. The letters of Paul were written to meet definite acute situations in the life of the Pauline churches. When those situations passed, the interest in the letters diminished for the next couple of generations. *The Gospels of Matthew, Mark, Luke*, and even *Acts* show no knowledge of the letters of Paul.

The Revelation of John reflects them greatly. It opens with a collection of Christian letters to the seven churches in Asia Minor. They were most likely published as a collection and published as an introduction to the Revelation. Ephesians might have served as a general introduction to the seven letters, because of its general content.

A letter from Clement of Rome to the Corinthians, written about 95 AD, gives clear evidence of a knowledge of Paul's letter. This collection included Ephesians, 1 and 2 Corinthians, Romans, Galatians, Philippians, Colossians, 1 and 2 Thessalonians, and Philemon.

The rise of the Synoptic Gospels, *Mark, Luke and Matthew*, were written between 70–90 AD, and were followed soon after by the *Gospel of John* around 90, in which the gospel narrative was greatly influenced by the ideas found in Paul's letters. The *Gospel of John* was designed to meet the needs of the Greek public which had become the field of the Christian mission, and soon after its appearance, it was joined with the other three by 120 AD. By 150 AD the four Gospels, these "memoirs of the Apostles," were joined side by side with the Jewish Bible and read in services of public worship.

By 189/200 AD, the following were accepted as suitable to be read in public worship: 1 Peter, 1 John, the Revelation of John, the four Gospels, Jude, the Shepherd of Hermas, eventually the letters to Timothy and Titus, although these may have been written sometime in the second century. The Shepherd of Hermas, in a Latin version, was very popular and included in some collections as late as 300 AD.

LANGUAGES OF THE NEW TESTAMENT

There were four languages current in Palestine during the centuries when the books of the New Testament were written. Hebrew survived as the language of Hebrew worship and scholarship. Aramaic was the everyday language and was probably spoken by Jesus. Latin came with the Romans in the first century BC and was used in government and legal affairs. If anyone saw the movie "The Passion," directed by Mel Gibson, you may have noted that when Jesus was before Pontius Pilate, he spoke Latin. Greek was the language of commerce and literature. The *koine* of common Greek was a hybrid of local dialects.

The books of the New Testament were written entirely in Greek, sometime between 50 and 109 AD. The quality of Greek varies widely from the elevated *koine* of the book of Hebrews to the almost colloquial of the book of *Revelation*. The books of the New Testament also contain ample evidence of the multi-lingual culture of their readers. It shows up in the *Aramaic, Hebrew* and even *Latin* phrases and words. The most striking example shows up in John's account of Jesus' crucifixion, in the multi-lingual sign affixed to the cross—written in Hebrew, Latin, and Greek.

THE GOSPEL OF MARK

One of the pivotal events in the history of Christianity occurred when a Christian put pen to papyrus and wrote in Greek, "The beginning of the good news of Jesus Christ, the son of God" (Mark 1:1). The name of the first century Christian who wrote "The Gospel According to Mark" is uncertain. However, Papias, bishop of Hierapolis, around 120 AD, identified him as John Mark, a young associate of the apostle Peter.[8]

Papias wrote this in his work called *Expositions of the Oracles of the Lord*, as contained in the works of Eusebius. Papias was attributed as being a "hearer" of John and companion of Polycarp. "Mark became the interpreter of Peter and he wrote down accurately, but not in order, as much as he remembered of the sayings and doings of Christ . . . Mark made no mistake when he thus wrote down some things as he remembered them; for he made it his special care to omit nothing of what he heard and to make no false statement therein."[9]

The Fourth Gospel is that of John, one of the disciples. "When his fellow disciples and bishops exhorted him, he said, 'Fast with me for three days from today, and then let us relate to each other whatever may be revealed to each of us.' On the same night it was revealed to Andrew, one of the Apostles, that John should narrate all things in his own name as they remembered them."[10] There

---

8. Huber, *Bible through the Ages*, 166.
9. Bettenson, *Documents of Christian*, 39.
10. Bettenson, *Documents of Christian*, 40.

is some speculation that John Mark was the unidentified youth recounted in Mark 14:51: "And a young man followed him, with nothing but a linen cloth about his body; and they seized him, but he left the linen cloth and ran away naked."

No other mention of this incident is found in the other Gospels. Some scholars think that the Last Supper was held in the upper room of the house of John Mark's mother, also named Mary, who possibly was the sister of Mary, the mother of Jesus (Acts 12:12). Such an incident in passing seems to be known only to Mark. If so, this might explain why Peter took young John Mark with him as his companion. Mark was also the cousin of Barnabas.[11]

Papias wrote that, "After their departure, Mark, the disciple and interpreter of Peter, himself handed down to us in writing the substance of Peter's preaching. Luke, the disciple of Paul, set down in a book the gospel preached by his teacher. Then John, the disciple of the Lord, who also leaned on his breast, produced his gospel, while he was living at Ephesus in Asia."[12]

The Gospel of Mark is the shortest of the four and most of its content is also found in Matthew and Luke. There are only twenty-four verses in Mark that are not reproduced in Matthew and Luke. It is straightforward with little of the "storytelling" characteristic found in Matthew and Luke. One-third of the Gospel deals with the last week of Jesus' life. It is generally accepted that the Gospel was written sometime before 70 AD while some date it as early as 50 AD.[13]

THE GOSPEL OF MATTHEW

The first book in the New Testament was accepted and canonized as having been written by the apostle Matthew, also called Levi, a

---

11. Lindsell, *Harper Study Bible*.
12. Bettenson, *Documents of Christian*, 40.
13. Lindsell, *Harper Study Bible*, 1462.

former tax gatherer. Some scholars date the writing of this book around 60 AD while others date it later, around 80 or 90 AD.[14]

Papias wrote, "Matthew published this gospel among the Hebrews in their own tongue, when Peter and Paul were preaching the Gospel in Rome and founding the church there."[15] William Barclay writes that there are two main characteristics of Matthew: "in no other Gospel is the teaching of Jesus so systematically assembled and gathered together. And it is preeminently the gospel which is concerned to show us Jesus as the man born to be king."[16]

The importance of this Gospel is shown by the fact that it is placed first. The early Christians quoted more from Matthew than from the other three Gospels. The author was Jewish, and he was writing for Jewish readers. It is closely related to the Old Testament and serves as a transition between the two Testaments. In its genealogy of Jesus, it directly traces Jesus back to Abraham, through David. It is traced through Jesus' father, Joseph. Matthew begins with the birth of Jesus, continues through his baptism, and follows Jesus through his teachings and works. It concludes with the Last Supper, the betrayal, arrest, crucifixion, and finally, the resurrection.

THE GOSPEL OF LUKE

It is generally accepted that Luke, whom Paul called "the beloved physician," is the author of this Gospel. Luke is not a Jew. He accompanied Paul on his journeys and acted as Paul's physician. Luke begins his Gospel in the temple with a relative of Mary.

Luke's prologue explains why he is writing his Gospel (read Luke 1:1–4). As with Matthew, he has a genealogy of Jesus; however, the ancestors are different from those of Matthew and he traces Jesus' lineage, not to Abraham, but to Adam, "the son of God." There is a birth narrative, as in Matthew; however, the visitors to the manger were shepherds, not Magi from the East. No star, no

---

14. Lindsell, *Harper Study Bible*, 1462.
15. Bettenson, *Documents of the Christian Church*, 39.
16. Barclay, *Gospel of Luke*, x.

flight into Egypt. No threat from Herod. Next, we see Jesus in the temple, on his eighth day, to be circumcised. One of the sources for this information was from Mary, herself. We read in Luke 2:19, "But Mary kept all these things, pondering them in her heart."

As in Matthew, we follow Jesus through his ministry. His words and works are recorded. Luke wrote that Jesus "came down with them and stood on a level place" (Luke 6:17) and proceeded to proclaim what Matthew called "The Sermon on the Mount." Luke also recounts the events of the last week—the plot to kill Jesus, the Last Supper, the prayer in the garden, the arrest, the trial, and the crucifixion. Luke ends his Gospel with the ascension of Jesus. We will see this event repeated in the first of the *book of Acts*.

THE SYNOPTIC GOSPELS

The first three Gospels—Matthew, Mark, and Luke—are usually known as the *Synoptic Gospels*. The word *synoptic* comes from two Greek words, *syn* and *optikos*, together meaning "able to be seen together." These three Gospels each gives an account of the same events in Jesus' life. Broadly speaking, their material is the same and their arrangement is the same. It is therefore possible to set them down in three parallel columns, read them together, and to compare them with each other.[17]

Matthew and Luke hesitate to attribute human emotions of anger and grief to Jesus, and almost shudder to think that Jesus ever was angry.[18] The three all recount the final days of Jesus— Last Supper, arrest, crucifixion, and resurrection. (Although some scholars think that Mark 16:9–20 was a later addition.)

Matthew and Luke tell of the birth of Jesus—Mark begins with the baptism of Jesus. Matthew and Luke also include this. Matthew, Mark, and Luke recount the Last Supper of Jesus with the sharing of the bread and wine (the Eucharist).

---

17. Barclay, *Gospel of Luke*, x.
18. Barclay, *Gospel of Luke*, x.

THE GOSPEL OF JOHN

John makes no mention of the birth, the baptism, or the Last Supper. In fact, he substitutes the washing of the disciples' feet for the act of communion. John begins with an introduction to Jesus' prehuman existence: "In the beginning was the Word" (John 1:1). Unlike the other Gospels, this Gospel names its author, "the disciple whom Jesus loved . . . who has written these things" (John 19:26, 21:24). Although he is not identified by name, all indications point to John the apostle.

The date most often suggested for the Fourth Gospel is the last decade of the first century AD, although some date it nearer to 70 AD.[19] Goodspeed places the writing of John's Gospel early in the second century, around 110 AD.[20] The field of Christianity was the Greek world and this new Gospel undertook to state Christian truth in a way attractive to the Greeks. It was a bold recasting and restatement of the new religion. A few years after its appearance, it was combined with the other three into a group of four—Matthew, Mark, Luke, and John. For a while though, Matthew remained a separate book.

John's explanation of his writing his Gospel sums up much of the method of the writing of the New Testament:

> Now Jesus did many other signs in the presence of the disciples, which are not written in this book; but these are written so that you may believe that Jesus is the Christ, the Son of God, and that believing you may have life in His name. (John 20; 30)

> This is the disciple who is bearing witness to these things, and who has written these things; and we know that his testimony is true. There are also many other things which Jesus did; however, were every one of them to be written, I suppose that the world itself could not contain the books that would be written. (John 21:24-25)

---

19. Lindsell, *Harper Study Bible*, 1582. Cadbury, "New Testament," 37; "If we should add a fourth period of equal length (about 96-128) we should assign to it probably to the Gospel of John."

20. Goodspeed, *How Came the Bible?*, 64.

CHAPTER 5 STUDY GUIDE

How long were the Jews independent of foreign rule before Jesus? _____

In what year did the Romans take control of Judea? _____

How did Herod become king? _____

What was one major accomplishment of Herod? _____

Who served as Judge of Judea? _____

The Jewish "parliament" or legislature was known as _____.

Herod's most infamous act was _____.

Rome's most widely known governor of Judea was _____.

The earliest Christians used _____ for Scripture and guidance.

The earliest Christian writings were written on _____.

Before the original writings wore out they were _____ many times. They were meant to be _____.

The first Christian writings to be used in churches were _____.

Matthew, Mark, and Luke show no knowledge of _____.

However, the writings of _____ show great dependence on Paul's letters.

The Synoptic Gospels are _____, _____, and _____.

The Synoptic Gospels were written around _____.

Many scholars think John was written around _____.

The Development of the New Testament: The Gospels

The Gospel of Matthew was written specifically for _____.

Whereas, John was written for _____.

Although the writers of the New Testament spoke _____, they wrote their books and letters in _____.

By 200 AD the books accepted as the Christian writings were:

_____, _____,
_____, _____,
_____, _____,
_____, and _____.

The best use of the Greek language is found in _____.

In addition to speaking Aramaic, Jesus probably spoke _____.

There are incidents of other languages in the New Testament. What are several of these? _____, _____, and _____.

Many scholars think the Last Supper was held _____.

Mark was the cousin of _____ and through him became a companion of _____ and _____.

Most of Mark's Gospel is found in _____ and _____.

The most quoted and the preeminent Gospel is _____.

Matthew traces Jesus' genealogy back to _____. Luke traces it back to _____.

What two important things do we know about Luke? _____ and he was _____.

Matthew indicates that _____ were visitors to Jesus' birth, while Luke mentions _____.

John makes no mention of _____, _____, and the _____.

One of the key sources of information about Jesus is _____.

Sometime after _____ the four Gospels were combined with Paul's writings to form the first "New Testament." However: Matthew's Gospel remained a separate book.

6

The Development of the New Testament: The Other Writings

Previously we saw that in the development of the Hebrew Scriptures, which we have come to call the *Old Testament,* many centuries passed during which oral stories and records were told and retold before they were collected and written down. Also, these writings did not attain the status of "Scripture" until 90 AD. We also saw that what the New Testament writers refer to as "Scripture" were these Hebrew writings.

We find a similar pattern in the development of the *New Testament,* except it occurred over decades rather than millennia. The first things to be written by the Christians were the letters of Paul. He wrote them to help lead the people in his new and struggling churches to a sounder view of their new religious experience to which he had introduced them. "He had no idea of producing a literature, still less a scripture. His writings were just personal or group letters, designed to produce an immediate practical effect."[1]

---

1. Weiss, *Earliest Christianity,* 3.

THE EPISTLES OF PAUL

The history of primitive Christianity is usually written as the history of St. Paul. He is the most significant personality of this period. His figure is the most brightly illumined. In his letters, he himself still speaks to us, and even in the *Acts of the Apostles* he is the character which strongly holds our attention.[2] The most authentic writings of Paul were all composed before the fall of Jerusalem; they show the apostle in a relation of constant contact with the primitive community."[3]

The letters of Paul were written between 50 and 62 AD. They were read and circulated for a while and then fell into disuse. The earliest Gospels, which came out between 70 and 90 AD, show no acquaintance with them. Paul had a very definite view of Christ as the pre-existent Messiah, the embodiment of divine Wisdom. Only John's writings reflect this.[4]

The first words written that are part of the New Testament are these: "Paul, Silvanus, and Timothy, to the church of the Thessalonians in God the Father and the Lord Jesus Christ: Grace to you and Peace" (1 Thess 1:1).

The Letter to the Thessalonians was the first letter of Paul and the first writing that was to become part of The New Testament. Paul was accompanied by his companions Timothy and Silas (Silvanus). Paul wrote what many scholars believe to be his *First Letter to the Thessaloians.*[5] By his own admission, Paul was not an impressive speaker, but most of his success was as a letter writer. He used these well-crafted letters to communicate his teachings to the widely scattered congregations and to deal with their problems.

Paul usually dictated his letters to a scribe. When he did write in his own hand he called attention to that fact. "I Paul write this greeting with my own hand. Remember my fetters. Grace be with you" (Col 4:18). "I Paul write this greeting with my own hand"

2. Weiss, *Earliest Christianity*, 3.
3. Weiss, *Earliest Christianity*, 3.
4. Goodspeed, *How Came the Bible?*, 59.
5. Huber, *Bible through the Ages*, 150.

(1 Cor 16:21). See also 2 Thessalonians 3:17. The problems Paul dealt with were immediate, local, and sometimes personal, which he handled directly and strongly.

It was not until after the appearance of *Luke-Acts* that anyone seems to have thought of collecting what letters of Paul's could be found. It was probably the account of Paul in the Acts that stirred somebody to hunt up the surviving letters and publish them.

There are specific needs and problems in the congregation. Paul calls for unity and also he addresses several social issues. Paul's *Letter to the Galatians* is an eloquent, often forceful defense of spiritual authority. He expresses his gratitude for their support of him, then he goes to the heart of the matter for which he is writing: "I am astonished that you are so quickly deserting the one who called you in the grace of Christ" (Gal 1:6) He then gives an account of his travels and life, reminding the readers that he has been called of God to bring the gospel to the gentiles.

The Letter to the Philippians is Paul's "love letter" to the first church he founded in Europe. His first convert there was Lydia, a prominent businesswoman, and a gentile attracted to Judaism. Most likely a synagogue met in her home. Paul wrote this from prison while awaiting trial in Ephesus.

Paul evidently wrote four letters to the church at Corinth. He stayed there a year and a half before returning to Palestine. Of the four letters Paul wrote to the Corinthians, the first is lost (1 Cor 5:9). He wrote a second letter in response to their inquiry about living the Christian life. There was also news about factionalism and immorality in Corinth.

Before leaving for Jerusalem, Paul wrote a letter to the church in Rome, introducing himself and requesting hospitality. The letter is an expression of Paul's faith and passionate trust in Jesus. He expressed his eagerness to visit the Roman Christians before going on to Spain. But first he must return to Jerusalem with a relief offering he had collected in Macedonia to help the Christians in Jerusalem.

From Corinth, Paul returned to Jerusalem. While there he took a gentile believer into the temple, beyond the court of the gentiles. In so doing Paul was arrested. This began his eventual journey to Rome. While in Rome, Paul wrote his "prison letters" to *Colossians* and *Philemon*.

The *Letter to the Colossians* deals with a troublemaker who is trying to teach a combination of Judaism and extreme self-denial. Paul urges the church to remain focused on Christ alone. He also wrote a letter to the Colossian Christian, *Philemon,* urging him to free his slave, Onesimus. The *Letter to the Ephesians* comments on and expands what is said in the *Letter to the Colossians* and may have been a cover letter. Paul also wrote this while in prison in Ephesus.

In his *Letter to the Corinthians* (1 Cor,, that is) are two of the most eloquent passages in the New Testament: *1 Corinthians 13* is a reminder that the greatest virtue is love (αγαπη, *agape*). This is selfless love that is focused on others. Also *1 Corinthians 15* is one of the highest claims for the resurrection of believers (1 Cor 15:51–58).

The small letters to *Philemon, Timothy*, and *Titus* are considered Paul's pastoral letters, written to a specific person for a particular purpose.

THE ACTS OF THE APOSTLES

It is safe to assume that Luke aligns himself with his predecessors. "It seemed good to me also, having followed all things closely for some time to write an orderly account" (Luke 1:3). Both in the Gospel and in Acts the material itself suggested and provided an intention.[6] It is safe to assume that Luke was carrying forward in his version of events the prevailing motives with which they had been handed down. His own purpose must have been minor and secondary.[7] Frank Stagg follows the theme of "an unhindered gospel" moving the story of Jesus across religious, social, political, and geographic barriers.[8] The final words of *Acts* are, "And he lived there two whole years at his own expense and welcomed all who

---

6. Cadbury, "New Testament," 300.
7. Cadbury, "New Testament, 31.
8. Stagg, *Book of Acts*, 266.

came to him, preaching the kingdom of God and teaching about the Lord Jesus Christ quite openly and unhindered" (28:30–31).

The title "*Acts of the Apostles*" was apparently the work of a copyist and not the author, Luke.[9] The book was written no earlier than about 59 or 60 AD.[10] Luke includes the arrest of Paul and his imprisonment in Rome, but he does not mention Paul's execution. However, Luke was more interested in issues than personalities. He leaves the fate of many of the apostles unknown, as this was not his primary purpose. Irenaeus, bishop of Antioch in 185 AD, "explicitly mentioned Luke as the author of the Gospel and Acts."[11] Luke is also mentioned in *1 Clement* (95 AD), the *Epistle of Barnabas*, (100 AD), the *Shepherd of Hermas* (100–110 AD), and Ignatius (115 AD), and the *Epistle of Polycarp* (120 AD).

The *Acts of the Apostles* was also an attempt by Luke to bring together the followers of Peter (Jewish Christians) and those of Paul (Gentile believers). The Jewish Roman War (70 AD) brought on a major crisis for Jews and Christians. The final break of the Christians from the synagogue and the turning of the Jews from Christianity no doubt were hastened by this war.[12]

It is clear that the New Testament writers were not slaves to verbatim reporting of speeches. They were concerned to correctly reproduce the substance of a speech, or even to interpret a speech, but they were not concerned to satisfy modern standards of writing.

PETER, JAMES, AND JUDE

James is a manual of Christian behavior and ethics. Its authorship is uncertain. Who is the "James" mentioned as the author? As late

---

9. See Stagg, *Book of Acts*, 7; "All scholars, except those denying Lukan authorship recognize that the author of Acts was a participant in much that belongs to the latter half of the book, but was not an eyewitness of that which belongs to the earlier half."

10. Stagg, *Book of Acts*, 20. IBID

11. Stagg, *Book of Acts*, 20.

12. Stagg, *Book of Acts*, 22.

as the fourth century there was divided opinion on the authorship. If this is James of Jerusalem, brother of Jesus, then it was written before 64 AD, the date of James' execution. Some think it was the first New Testament writing, dating in 45 AD. Others date it much later, toward the end of the first century or the beginning of the second. The "dispersion" may or may not refer to the *diaspora*, or the scattering of the Jews from Jerusalem at the time of its 70 AD destruction. *James* had a very hard time getting into the *New Testament*. When it did come to be regarded as Scripture, it was still spoken of with a certain reserve and suspicion, and even as late as the sixteenth century Luther would gladly have banished it from the New Testament altogether.

In the Latin-speaking church it is not until the middle of the fourth century that *James* emerges in the writings of the church fathers at all. Tertullian, a great quoter of Christian writings, has 7,258 New Testament quotations in his writings, but none from *James*.[13] The first mention of *James* in Latin was in 350 AD. It was included not with the other Scriptures, but in a collection of religious tracts written by early church fathers.

If *James* was so controversial, how did it ever get in the New Testament? The great influence that moved *James* into the level of Scripture was Jerome, who included it in his *Vulgate* version of the *New Testament*. Jerome accepted the writing as Scripture, but still had some doubts about its author. William Barclay writes, "So then, in the early Church no one really questioned the value of *James,* but in every branch of the church it was late in emerging and in every branch it was viewed with some questions."[14] In 1546, the Council of Trent of the Roman Catholic Church laid down once and for all the Roman Catholic Bible. James was included but only as *deuterocanonical* writing, that is a book that had some difficulty being accepted. Although *James* was accepted in the Roman Catholic Bible (Jerome's *Vulgate),* among Protestants, especially Luther, the book of *James* was a "strawy" Epistle.

---

13. Barclay, *Letters of James*, 3.
14. Barclay, *Letters of James*, 3.

First Peter is one of the most loved letters in the New Testament. *First Peter, 2 Peter,* and *Jude* are usually grouped together in commentaries. *First Peter* is addressed to the strangers scattered abroad throughout Pontus, Galatia, Cappadocia, Asia, and Bythinia. The authorship is much in dispute. One of the principal reasons is the excellent Greek in which it is written. It seems impossible that a Palestinian fisherman could write such beautiful Greek. F. W. Beare writes that, "The epistle is quite obviously the work of a man of letters, skilled in all the devices of rhetoric, and able to draw on an extensive, and even learned vocabulary." The writer "writes some of the best Greek in The New Testament.," according to Beare. But the Epistle itself supplies an answer to this problem: Peter himself says, "By Silvanus I have written briefly" (1 Pet 5:12). Silvanus was more than just a secretary, he evidently formed the style of the writing itself.

Second Peter is most likely written by someone other than Peter the apostle. The style of writing, the vocabulary, tone, and thought are different.[15] Even the early church fathers were skeptical about the authorship and thus reluctant to accept the writing as Scripture. The earliest mention of *2 Peter* was in Origen. While he accepted the writing he mentioned that many were doubtful of it. The date of authorship was most likely in the first half of the second century.[16] The book of *2 Peter* finally gained acceptance when Jerome included it in his *Vulgate,* in 385 AD.

Jude may have been written by the brother of Jesus, although there was some doubt. However, there was enough support to include the writing that it became a part of the canon. *Jude* and *2 Peter* seemed to have some connection in that the one influenced the other, but which one was first written remains uncertain.

---

15. Cranfield, *I & II Peter,* 148.
16. Cranfield, *I & II Peter,* 149.

THE WRITER OF HEBREWS

The longest of the non-Pauline Epistles in *Hebrews* is a detailed argument for the Christian message that exalts Jesus as the "great high Priest" (4:14), not only as the priest who offers sacrifice, but also as the sacrifice which takes away the sins of the world.

Early tradition ascribes *Hebrews* to Paul, but nowhere does the text mention Paul. Also, the style of writing is so different from Paul's that even in ancient times many scholars recognized that it did not come from Paul.[17] Suggested authors are Luke, Apollos, Barnabas, or Priscilla. The date and place from which it was written are not certain. Its form is more of a dissertation than a letter. The closing greeting does not identify the recipients of the letter.

The author seemed to be personally acquainted with his readers and hoped someday to be reunited with them. The occasion for the writing was the severe danger from persecution. The readers seem to have been Jewish Christians who were in danger of abandoning their faith and lapsing back into Judaism, thus running the risk of apostasy. So he exhorts them to hold fast to their confession in Christ as Savior and Lord (14:14; 10:23).

THE REVELATION OF JOHN

The writer is known simply as "John." No reference to his being the apostle. Most scholars believe he was a leader in the church at Ephesus known as "John the Elder." There is record of such a leader in the church who was so outspoken in his proclamation of Jesus that the governor banished him to the Isle of Patmos. He identifies himself as a "servant" and "fellow sufferer." He evidently knew the writings of Paul as he addressed his writing to the seven churches which Paul had founded. The style is *apocalyptic,* that is a vision full of symbolic images which tell of future events surrounding the cataclysmic end of the world and the judgment of God. It was written sometime around 95 AD.

---

17. Huber, *Bible through the Ages*, 156.

OTHER EARLY CHRISTIAN WRITINGS

Several other writings appeared about the same time as the Gospel of John and the Revelation. They were read in public worship and recommended as good Christian writing but were not included in the Western Church canon. Again, *canon* originally means "a reed or measuring rod."[18] Among these were *the Preaching of Peter, 2 Peter, the Gospel of Peter, Interpretations of Papias, the Epistle of the Apostles, the Apology of Justin,* and *the Shepherd of Hermas.*

THE FIRST NEW TESTAMENT

Around 175 AD a movement was started to collect the writings that would be considered authoritative as Christian Scripture. For our purposes, the books that we now have in our *New Testament* were finally collected and approved. There were many different collections, but it was finally Jerome's version in the *Vulgate*, written in Latin in 367 AD, that became the standard Bible of Western Europe—and is still that of the Roman Catholic Church. The Eastern Orthodox and the Coptic Scriptures are mostly like the version of the Western Church but omit several books and included still others.

SUMMARY

What began as stories and traditions of thousands of years past and continued with the collection of laws, prophecies, poetry, histories, and finally with letters and Gospels, were officially combined by 367 AD to make our Scriptures—the *Holy Bible*. It was a process filled with discussion, debate, research, and some hostilities. But can we say it was a process overseen by the Holy Spirit to bring us a book in which we might understand the workings of the One True God? As several have written, "History is His story."

---

18. Smith, How We Got, 3.

CHAPTER 6 STUDY GUIDE

The Old Testament writings attained the status of "Scripture" in _____.

The first Christian writings were _____.

These were written to _____.

Early Christian history is mainly the history of _____.

Paul is the most important figure in_____.

The letters of Paul were written between _____ and _____.

_____ was Paul's first letter.

Only _____ Gospel reflects knowledge of Paul.

Paul's two traveling companions were _____ and _____.

Paul was called of God to do what? _____

Paul founded his first European church in _____ and _____ was his first convert.

When did people start collecting Paul's letters? _____

Paul wrote ____ letters to the Corinthians. We have only ____.

Why was Paul arrested in Jerusalem? _____

Paul had hoped to go to _____, which was at the end of the world.

Why did Paul return to Jerusalem? _____

Where was Paul when he wrote his "prison letters"? _____

What are the two greatest writings of Paul in the Bible?

1.
2.

Who was Philemon? _____

The Development of the New Testament: The Other Writings

The *Acts of the Apostles* was an attempt by Luke to bring together what two groups? _____ and _____.

James was thought for many years to have been written by: _____

Why did James have a hard time being accepted in the *canon*?

James finally gained acceptance when he was included in the _____ of _____.

This was in the year _____.

Who called *James* a "strawy" Epistle? _____.

If Paul did not write *Hebrews*, who might have?

1. _____
2. _____
3. _____
4. _____

Hebrews focuses on Jesus as the _____.

He is also the _____.

The occasion for writing *Hebrews* was _____.

Jewish Christians were thinking of reverting to Judaism. What do we call it when a Christian joins another religion? _____

Most scholars today believe that _____ wrote *Revelation*. He was a leader of the church in _____.

The style of writing in *Revelation* is called _____. It is characterized by _____.

The New Testament, as we have it, was finally accepted by _____ in the Western (Roman) church.

Can we say that the formation of the New Testament and the Bible was a process overseen by _____?

And herein is the "inspiration" of the Bible: the collection of God—directed writings through three thousand years, in multiple languages, through discussions, arguments, councils, ex-communication and persecutions. "Herein is the Word of God."

7

Putting it All Together

We have seen how the Old Testament developed and became what we have in today's Bible. We have also seen how the New Testament came together. So now we have the Bible. Or do we? Let's say that now the struggle begins on what goes into and what is omitted from what we call the Bible. In reality, Christians will not have a definitive Bible for two or three hundred more years.

Henry Cadbury writes: "The New Testament is a collection of some twenty seven early Christian writings. This collection has been separately treated since the third or fourth century. But in reality, it is only a fragment of a larger and more varied amount of material that sundry Christians of the early days put in written form."[1]

DISPUTES OVER THE CANON

First of all, let us define what we mean by "canon." Let us immediately know that "canon" is not a weapon. *Canon* is derived from a Hebrew and Greek word meaning "reed" or "straw." So, it means something straight, hence also a rule, or something ruled or measured. It came

---

1. Cadbury, "New Testament and Early Christian Literature," 32.

to be applied to Scriptures, to denote that they contain the authoritative rule of faith and practice, the standard of doctrine and duty.[2]

In the first three centuries of the Christian era there were several "canons," or collections of writings that various groups considered authoritative enough to be used in public worship. These collections varied from one Christian center to others.

By 150 AD there were several centers of Christian churches. The Eastern Church centers were:

- Jerusalem, although it had been greatly destroyed in 70 AD
- Antioch
- Alexandria
- Byzantium (Constantinopal) after 400 AD
- Ephesus
- Ethiopia (Adis Ababa)

The Western Church centers were:

- Rome
- Spain
- Carthage
- Southern Gaul

Each center had its favorite writings that they considered "Scripture." All agreed on the four Gospels, the writings of Paul, the Hebrew Scriptures, *1 Peter*, books that remained in doubt until at least the third and fourth centuries were *2 Peter, 2 and 3 John, James, Jude*, and the *Revelation*.

Origen (185–254) mentions the four Gospels, the *Acts*, the thirteen Paulines, *1 Peter, 1 John*, and *Revelation*, as acknowledged by all; he says that *Hebrews, 2 Peter, 2 and 3 John, James, Jude*, the *Epistle of Barnabas*, the *Shepherd of Hermas*, the *Didache*, and the "*Gospel according to the Hebrews*" were disputed by some.[3]

---

2. See "Canon."
3. Bruce, "Canon of the New Testament," 4.

Putting it All Together

Origen grew up in Alexandria, the son of Christian parents. His father was a martyr in the persecution by Septimus Severus in 202. He was the most familiar with the Scriptures of any Christian writers in the church at that time.[4]

Eusebius (265 to 340), bishop of Caesarea, mentions all the books in our New Testament except James, Jude, 2 Peter, and 2 and 3 John—which were disputed by some but acknowledged by the majority. In 325, Emperor Constantine asked Eusebius to provide Bibles for church use in Constantinople. Eusebius had to decide which writings went into the Bibles. He divided the writings into three categories:[5]

1. Writings that were already accepted by all the churches: the *four Gospels, Acts of the Apostles*, thirteen letters of Paul, *1 John*, and *1 Peter*

2. Writings that were somewhat in dispute: *James, 2 Peter, Jude, 2 and 3 John, Hebrews,* and *Revelation*

3. Writings that were viewed as Scripture by many but which Eusebeus did not accept: *Gospels of Peter, Thomas, Matthias, Acts of Andrew, of Paul, of John, Shepherd of Hermas*, the *Epistle of Barnabas*, the *Didache.*

In spite of the break with Judaism, the Christians did not repudiate the authority of the *Old Testament,* but following the practice of Jesus and the apostles, received it as the word of God.

The Orthodox Church encompasses all those communions in the Eastern domain of the Empire: Egypt, Ethiopia, Syria, Armenia, Greece, Arabia, Persia, and India.

The Eastern Orthodox Church belief about Holy Scripture is that we must be fully aware from within the holy tradition that the Bible of the Old Testament and the New Testament are Scripture. "Tradition," is a live, personal encounter with Christ our Lord in the Holy Spirit. Tradition then not only is kept by the Church—it lives

---

4. Walker et al., *History of Christian*, 74.
5. Huber, *Bible through the Ages*, 213.

in the Church, it is the life of the "Holy Spirit in the Church. The Bible is then the supreme expression of God's revelation to man."[6]

Strictly speaking, there never was a "Bible" in the Orthodox Church. At least not as we commonly think of the Bible as a single volume book. Instead the various "books" of the Bible are found scattered throughout several service books located either on the holy altar itself, or at the canter's stand. The church is not based on the Bible, rather the Bible is a product of the church. For the first few centuries of the church no one could have put their hands on a single volume called "the Bible."[7]

CRITERIA FOR ACCEPTANCE

The process by which the New Testament writings came to scriptural authority seems to have been one of analogy. The Old Testament was everywhere regarded as divinely authoritative. Christians could think no less of their own fundamental books. The question was an open one, however, as to which the canonical writings were.[8]

The whole process of developing the New Testament canon was not completed in the West until 400, and in the East until even later. The criterion by which a writing was accepted in the canon was that the writing was the work of an apostle or the immediate disciple of an apostle, thus representing apostolic teaching.

The churches would never be in absolute agreement on the New Testament canon. The Syrians used the *Peshitta* as their canon for another half century. The *Peshitta* is the *Aramaic* rendering of the Scriptures used by the Syrian Church. The Ethiopian Church continues to recognize a book of *Clement* and several other books in their canon.[9]

---

6. Serfes, *Holy Scripture*, 1.
7. Serfes, *Holy Scripture*, 1.
8. Walker, *History of Christian*, 59.
9. Huber, *Bible through the Ages*, 215.

REJECTED WRITINGS

There were many Christian writings by the end of the first century; some were acceptable for reading in public worship. Others were recommended for spiritual inspiration. Among these were: the *Apocalypse of Peter*, the *Gospel of Peter*, the *Gospel of Thomas*, the *Gospel of Matthias*, the *Acts of Andrew*, the *Acts of Paul*, the *Acts of John*, the *Shepherd of Hermas*, the *Epistle of Barnabas*, the *Didache*, and *1 and 2 Clement*.[10]

The *Didache* was discovered in the latter part of the nineteenth century. In English its title would be "The Teaching of the Lord to the Gentiles through the Twelve Apostles." It is an instruction book about the use of the sacraments and other church practices.[11]

ACCEPTED WRITINGS AND DATES OF ACCEPTANCE

Marcion, a wealthy ship owner in Pontus and a Christian leader, made frantic efforts to revive the writings of Paul and to throw aside the Old Testament around 140 AD. He preferred Luke to the other Gospels. He was the first man to try to formulate a Christian Scripture that could be used in public worship. He found the Old Testament repugnant. He felt that the God of the Old Testament was other than the God and Father of Jesus Christ. He had a following for his "canon," but was eventually declared a heretic.[12]

The development of a canon of New Testament books was also the work of the later second century. The earliest designation of a passage from the Gospels as "Scripture" was about 131, by the so-called Barnabas,[13] and of a quotation from Paul about 110–17 by Polycarp.[14]

Egyptian Christianity was inclined to accept as Scripture almost anything it found edifying. It was too easily impressed by writings

---

10. Huber, *Bible through the Ages*, 212.
11. Cadbury, "Early Christian," 40.
12. Goodspeed, *How Came the Bible?*, 66.
13. Goodspeed, *How Came the Bible?*, 66.
14. Goodspeed, *How Came the Bible?*, 66.

that claimed apostolic authorship. The Egyptian Christians included a great deal more in their Scriptures at the end of the second century.[15]

THE FINAL WESTERN (ROMAN) CANON

In 367, Athanasius lays down the twenty-seven books of our New Testament as canonical. He was followed shortly by Jerome and Augustine in the Western Church. The process in the East took longer. It was not until 508 AD that 2 Peter, 2 and 3 John, Jude, and the Revelation were included in the Syriac Bible. Athanasius' canon was accepted by the Roman church and ratified by the pope in 405. Carthage formally affirmed its acceptance of this canon in 419.

In conclusion, we can summarize all we have considered with three quotations from the Holy Scriptures:

> Inasmuch as many have undertaken to compile a narrative of the things which have been accomplished among us, just as they were delivered to us by those who from the beginning were eyewitnesses and ministers of the word, it seemed good to me also, having followed all things closely for some time past, to write an orderly account for you, most excellent Theophilus, that you may know the truth concerning the things of which you have been informed. (Luke 1:1–4)

Now Jesus did many other signs in the presence of the disciples, which are not written in this book; but these are written that you may believe that Jesus is the Christ, the Son of God, and that believing you may have life in his name. (John 20:30–31)

> This is the disciple who is bearing witness to these things, and who has written these things; and we know that his testimony is true. But there are also many other things which Jesus did; were every one of them to be written, I suppose that the world itself could not contain the books that would be written. (John 21:24–25)

To God Be the Glory!

---

15. Goodspeed, *How Came the Bible?*, 66.

Putting it All Together

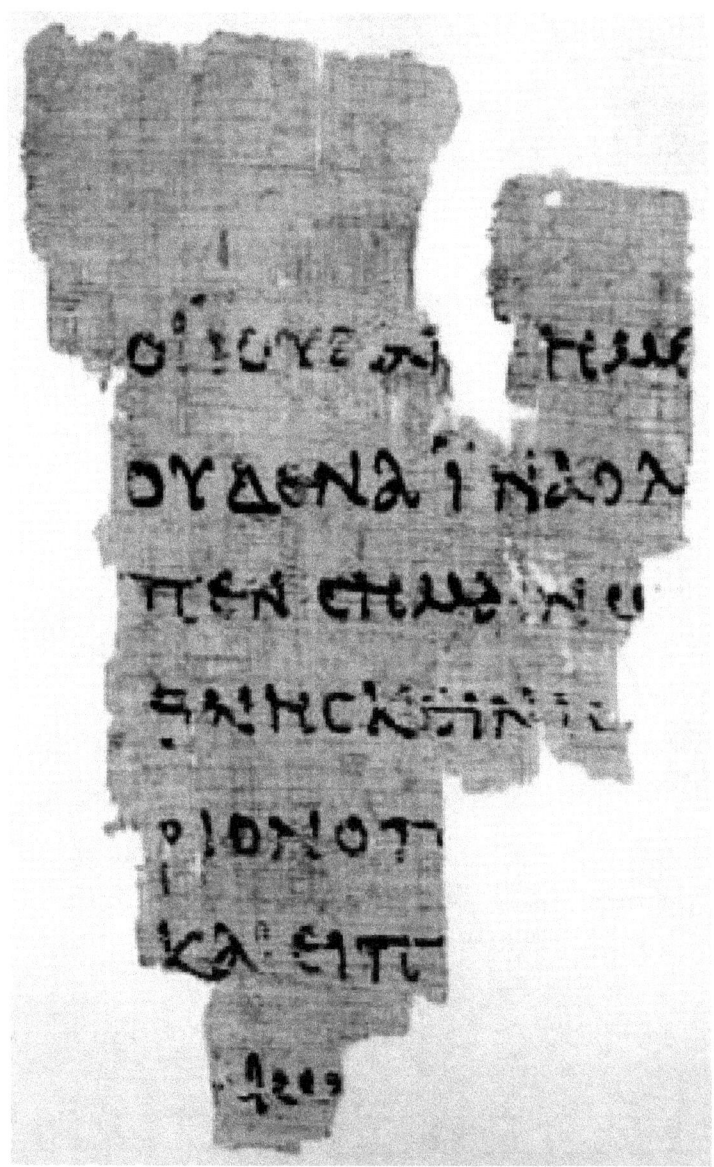

Ancient Fragment of New Testament

CHAPTER 7 STUDY GUIDE

The New Testament is _____.

By the word "canon" we mean _____.

In the first three centuries of the Christian church there were _____ canons.

By 150 several Christian centers in the Eastern Church were:

1.
2.
3.
4.

The major Christian center in the West was _____.

The Orthodox Church extends to _____.

In the Orthodox Church _____ is the supreme expression of God's revelation to man.

There was never _____ in the Orthodox Church.

The New Testament was not complete until _____.

A writing was acceptable in the canon if _____.

Some of the non-accepted Christian writings at the end of the first century were: _____, _____, _____, _____, _____, and _____.

It took several centuries before the books of _____, _____, _____, _____, _____, and _____ were accepted in the New Testament.

_____ was a wealthy ship builder and leader in the church. He made the first collection of writings to be used in public worship.

This man was also strongly against the _____ being a part of Christian Scripture.

Athanasius accepts the twenty-seven books of our New Testament in _____.

He was followed by _____ and _____.

Athanacius' collection of writings was ratified by the pope in _____.

In _____, Carthage finally affirmed this collection as Scripture.

This is the official canon of the New Testament in the Western Church and is the basis for the Bible we use as our guide and standard of Christian faith.

The Bible we use today is different in some respects from the Catholic Bible, the Coptic, Syrian, and Indian (MarThoma) Scriptures. But all contain the four Gospels, the Acts of the Apostles, and the thirteen letters of Paul. Yet with all our differences, we are single in our confession that "Jesus Christ is Lord."

Front Cover of Jerome's Vulgate

8

Jerome and the Latin Vulgate

INTRODUCTION

By the early fourth century a confusing variety of Scriptures in Latin and other languages was in circulation throughout the young church with many of them containing inaccuracies and incompetent translations. As Jerome later said, "There are almost as many forms of the text as there are copies."[1] He described his endeavor to revise his translation of the Gospels as one to "correct the mistakes by inaccurate translators and the blundering alterations of confident but ignorant critics, and further, all that has been inserted or changed by copyists more asleep than awake."[2]

JEROME

Eusebius Sophronius Hieronymus was born at Stridon in Dalmatia around 347 AD. He was of Illyrian ancestry and his native tongue

---

1. Huber, *Bible through the Ages*, 221.
2. Huber, *Bible through the Ages*, 221.

St. Jerome

was the Illyrian dialect, a proto language to the Albanian and Croatian languages, one of a number of indo-European languages spoken in the Balkans.³

He was not baptized until sometime between 360–66 AD, between the ages of thirteen and nineteen years. At this time in early church practice, baptism was administered to adults after a time

3. See "Jerome."

of instruction (catechism) and usually on Easter morning. The practice was normally by total immersion until the fourth and fifth centuries.[4] As a youth, he went to Rome with his friend Bonosus and was there baptized. As a student in Rome, Jerome was a typical schoolboy with many escapades and "wanton behavior" as students might do. But he felt tremendous grief after such incidents that for penance he would visit on Sundays the catacombs and sepulchers of the martyrs and apostles. These experiences would remind him of hell. Jerome was born of wealthy Christian parents who wished for their son the best education in philosophy and languages. After his baptism, he went to live on an island in the Adriatic where he studied rhetoric and philosophy. There Jerome learned Latin and some Greek.

Although initially skeptical of Christianity, he was eventually converted. He traveled with his friend Bonosus to Gaul and took up theological studies, where he translated a commentary on the *Psalms* and a treatise. Next came a stay of several months, or possibly years, in Aquileia (a city in Northern Italy of about one hundred thousand population at that time), where he made many Christian friends.

Some of these friends accompanied him when he set out in 373 on a journey through Asia Minor and into northern Syria. At Antioch he and his friends stayed for several years. There, two of his friends died and Jerome, himself, became seriously ill. During one of his illnesses (ca. 373–374) he had a vision that led him to lay aside his secular studies and devote himself to God. He retreated to the desert and assumed the life of a hermit and filled his days with the study of Hebrew as a means of distracting his mind from his love of classical Greek and Latin literature. He wrote, "However much I did penance, I always ended up by creeping back to Cicero or Plautus. Even if I suddenly pulled myself together and read the Bible. . . . I would close it again, repelled by its clumsiness."[5]

In 379 AD, Jerome left the desert and went to Antioch, then to Constantinople, to study with leading theologians. He continued

---

4. See "Baptism in Early Christianity."
5. Huber, *Bible through the Ages*, 220.

on to Rome where Pope Damasus appointed him his secretary. Impressed by Jerome's gifts as a biblical scholar, the pope commissioned him to produce a new Latin revision of the Bible.

In 382, Jerome, the greatest scholar of the Western Church, set about revising the Bible. He visited the East and spent a long time in Palestine, working on the Old Testament. He studied under the guidance of a converted Jew and was in contact with Jewish Christians in Antioch. About this time, he had copied for him a Hebrew Gospel of which fragments are preserved in his notes.[6] He was aware of doubts in the Western Church concerning the inclusion of the *book of Hebrews*.[7] Jerome translated part of this Gospel into Greek and it is known today as the *Gospel of the Hebrews*.[8]

When Jerome returned to Antioch in 378/379, he was ordained by Bishop Paulinus, apparently unwilling, and on the condition that he continue his ascetic life. Soon after, he went to Constantinople for two years to study the Scriptures under Gregory Naziazen. He then returned again to Rome, as secretary to Pope Damasus I and the leading Roman Christians.

He was given duties in Rome and he undertook a revision of the Latin Bible to be based on the Greek manuscripts of the New Testament. He also updated the *Psalter,* then at use in Rome, which was based on the *Septuagint*. Translating much of what became the *Latin Vulgate* would take many years and be his most important achievement.

In Rome he was surrounded by a circle of well-born and well-educated women, including some from the noblest patrician families, such as the widows, Lea, Marcella, and Paula, with their daughters Blaesilla and Eustochium. Their inclination towards the monastic life and Jerome's criticism of the secular clergy caused a growing hostility against him among the Roman clergy and their supporters.[9]

---

6. See "Jerome."
7. Goodspeed, *How Came the Bible?*, 84.
8. See "Jerome."
9. See "Jerome."

Soon after the death of his patron, Pope Damasus I (December 10, 384),[10] Jerome was forced from his position in Rome. He was accused of an improper relationship with the widow Paula. However, his letters were widely read and distributed throughout the Christian Empire. In August 385, he left Rome for good and returned to Antioch, accompanied by his brother Paulinian and several friends, to be followed later by the widows Paula and Eustochium. They also joined him in a pilgrimage with Bishop Paulinius to Jerusalem, Bethlehem, and Egypt.

Late in the summer of 388 he was back in Palestine and spent the remainder of his life working in a cave near Bethlehem, allegedly the very cave in which Jesus was born. Adequately provisioned by Paula and surrounded by a company of friends, he was active in literary production. These last thirty-four years of his life were probably the most important for his works: his version of the best of his scriptural commentaries, *Catalogue of Christian Authors* and *Dialogue against the Pelagians.*

It is reported that Jerome died near Bethlehem on September 30, 420. His remains, originally buried at Bethlehem, are said to have been taken to the basilica of Santa Maria Maggiore in Rome, though other places also claim his remains.

THE VULGATE

Prior to Jerome's *Vulgate,* all Latin translations of the *Old Testament* were based on the *Septuagint,* not the Hebrew. By 390, he started translating the Hebrew Bible from the Hebrew. He believed that the mainstream rabbinical Judaism had rejected the Septuagint as invalid Jewish scriptural texts because of what were ascertained as mistranslations along with its Hellenistic heretical elements. He completed this work by 405.

Jerome was initially charged by Pope Damasus I to revise the Old Latin text of the four Gospels from the best Greek texts, and

---

10. See "Jerome."

JEROME AND THE LATIN VULGATE

by the time the pope died in 384, he had completed the task. When Jerome was forced to leave Rome in 385, he settled in Bethlehem.

In Bethlehem, he found a surviving manuscript of the *Hexapla*, a comparison by columns of the various versions of the Old Testament arranged by Origen nearly 150 years previously. He put Latin translations from the *Hexapla-Septuagint* side by side in columns of the *Psalms* and later did other books.

But from 390–405, Jerome translated all thirty-nine books in the Hebrew Bible *from the Hebrew*, including a new translation of the *Psalms*. The *Vulgate* is usually credited with being the first translation of the Old Testament into Latin directly from the Hebrew *Tanakh*, (The Hebrew canonical Scriptures, the Christian Old Testament) instead of from the Latin.

Those books in the Greek Septuagint not found in the Hebrew Old Testament were, as he called them "non-canonical." However, Jerome did translate *Tobit* and *Judith* from the Aramaic; from the Greek he translated additions to *Esther* from the *Septuagint* and additions to *Daniel* from Theodocian; he also translated other books such as *Baruch, Letter of Jeremiah, Wisdom, Ecclesiasticus, 1* and *2 Maccabees* from the Old Latin. He translated other writings not found in either the Hebrew Bible or the Septuagint—the *Prayer of Manasses* and *Laodiceans*. Their style differs greatly from that of Jerome. Jerome included the *Letter to the Hebrews* and attributed it to Paul's authorship

RESPONSE TO THE VULGATE

While Jerome's Gospel translations were widely accepted early on, his Old Testament translations were far from universally popular. They drew strong opposition from other translators, some of whom were involved in ongoing debates with Jerome. Among the average church member, their preference for the familiar traditional text, which many of them knew by heart, was more appreciated than Jerome's new translation. Augustine also voiced opposition based on his belief that the Septuagint was inspired and Jerome's translation from the Hebrew was mistaken.[11] Eventually the new translation won the day and for centuries it was the only translation used by the Catholic Church.

Perhaps reflecting on the response of many to the translation of the *Revised Standard Version*, Robert M. Grant writes, "Many new versions are opposed by backward looking Christians, but few are greeted with the abuse which the Vulgate at first encountered. Jerome was called a forger and a betrayer of his religion."[12]

Jerome's version, the Latin Vulgate, became the standard Bible of Western Europe and is still that of the Catholic Church. And as we shall be seeing in the next chapters, Jerome's Vulgate is the foundation on which our current English language Bibles are built.

11. Grant, "History," 111.
12. Grant, "History," 111.

Jerome and the Latin Vulgate

CHAPTER 8 STUDY GUIDE

By the _____ century, many conflicting versions of the Bible contained _____.

Eusebius Sophronius Hieronymus is known in history as _____.

He was born in Dalmatia around the year _____.

He was _____ years old when baptized.

In the early church, most baptisms were held on _____ after a time of instruction.

The mode of baptism was _____.

As a schoolboy, Jerome's behavior was a typical one of wild behavior. As penance, Jerome would _____.

After his baptism Jerome _____ where he _____.

He traveled to _____, and then to _____. Several friends accompanied him on a tour through _____.

He stayed in _____ for several years, where two of his friends died from illness. Jerome was also ill there and during his illness _____.

He then retreated to _____. His spiritual conflict was between his love for _____ and for _____.

In the desert, he learned _____.

In 379, Jerome left the desert and went to _____, then to _____, where he studied with leading theologians. Then he went to Rome where _____ made him his secretary. Pope Damasus I commissioned him to _____.

By 832, Jerome was _____ in the Western Church.

Where on Earth Did the Bible Come From?

In Palestine and Jerusalem he studied the _____ working with _____ and _____.

Most Old Testament translators translated from _____, which was a Greek translation of the Hebrew.

Jerome translated directly from _____.

When he returned to Rome, he updated the Latin New Testament going to the _____.

He began his work on the Old Testament, which became the basis for the _____.

His association with a _____ and his support of the _____ drew opposition from the clergy and forced him to flee Rome.

He left Rome for good and returned to _____, accompanied by his brother and the group of widows.

After a trip to Jerusalem, Bethlehem and Egypt he returned to _____.

He spent the remaining thirty-four years of his life living in a cave and completing his work on the Latin Old Testament and other important documents. It is reported that Jerome died on _____.

His remains were originally interred at _____ but were reportedly taken to _____. Several locations claim his remains.

From _____ to _____ Jerome translated all thirty-nine books of the Old Testament into Latin directly from _____.

Jerome also included the disputed New Testament book of _____

Today the Vulgate is the _____ for all Bibles in the Western Church.

9

From Rome through Europe

The visible decline of the Roman Empire is usually reckoned from the death of Marcus Aurelius in 180, though its causes go back much further.[1] From a religious point of view, the close of the second century and the whole of the third centuries were an age of syncretism, a period of deepening religious feeling in which the mystery religions of the Orient—and Christianity also—made exceedingly rapid gains in the number of their adherents.[2] The growth of the church was extensive as well as intensive. By the beginning of the third century the church was rapidly advancing in Latin-speaking North Africa and, though more slowly, in Spain and Gaul, and was reaching, if not already in, Great Britain. It was growing among the people in Egypt and was well represented in Syrian-speaking Edessa. The church was also reaching into the higher classes of society.

Remember, all this and yet no set Christian Scripture. Due to the lack of a canon of Scripture there were developing controversies dealing mainly with the person of Christ. Was he more man than spirit? Was he more spirit than man? Was he man at all?

1. Walker, *History of Christian*, 78.
2. Walker, *History of Christian*, 78.

When Roman persecution ended with the ascendency of Constantine as emperor, the blending of the sacred and the secular continued at an accelerated pace. Some of this had already begun, but it now increased. As Christianity became established and Christians no longer lived under the threat of persecution, martyrdom ceased to be the ultimate expression of the faith. Consequently, Christians trying to achieve spiritual perfection began withdrawing from the world to take up a life of solitude, asceticism, and the contemplation of Scripture.[3]

> The low condition of the Church led to the growing importance of the ascetic life by serious-minded Christians. Above all, the formalization of public worship, which developed by the end of the third century led to a desire for a freer and more individual approach to God. Monasticism was soon to become formalized, but at first, was a breach in public worship and service. Initially it was a layman's movement.[4]

St. Anthony

3. Huber, *Bible through the Ages*, 226.
4. Walker, *History of Christian*, 1125.

Monasteries

The founder of Christian monasticism was Anthony. He was born in Koma, central Egypt, of Coptic parents about the year 250. At age twenty he was impressed by Christ's advice to the rich young man "to go and sell your possessions and give the proceeds to the poor."[5] About 270 he took up the ascetic life and eventually went to live in the ruins of an abandoned fortress near the Red Sea.[6] The Christian monastic movement originated in the late third century AD in the desert regions of Egypt. By that time there already existed a tradition of retreat to the desert by those seeking to escape a variety of social pressures.[7] Others followed Anthony's example. Hermits, or *anchorites*, some of them women, took up residence in caves, ruins, or other rude dwellings. They shed all material possessions, save those necessary for survival. Alone in the desert, they prayed, recited Scripture, worked, fasted, and maintained a constant vigil against the demonic spirits they believed to be all around them in the desert. As loosely organized communities of monks grew up around charismatic elders, the solitary tradition began to yield to a communal way of life.

The most influential rule in the West was that of Benedict of Nursia (480–540). Benedict's dicta partially drew on the rule that became the founding principles of Western monasticism. Other strong monastic influences were developed. Among the first was the Cistercians, begun by a Benedictine monk, Robert, of the monastery of Montier, with the strictest discipline. They combined prayer and devotion with work, a simple diet, and vows of silence. In spite of its austerity, the movement grew rapidly until, in 1278, there were more than seven hundred Cistercian houses.[8]

---

5. Matt 19:21.
6. Huber, *Bible through the Ages*, 227.
7. Huber, *Bible through the Ages*, 227.
8. The Monastery of The Holy Spirit in Conyers, Georgia is of the Cistercian Order, as is Gethsemane Monastery in Bardstown, Kentucky and St. Meinrad Monastery in Southern Indiana.

Another movement included Bernard of Clairvaux, and yet another monastic movement that endures up to today was begun by Francis of Assisi (the Franciscans). The Dominicans were started by Dominic, a native of Calaroga, Spain. Quite different from the peace-making Franciscans, the Dominicans became the "protectors of the faith" from among whom was given the task of supporting and providing leadership for the Inquisition.

Because there was no Bible in country after expanding country, the monasteries became the place where copies of the Latin Scriptures were translated into the languages of the people.

In the early fifth century, a monk known as Mesrop, decided to translate the Bible into Armenian, with the blessing of Bishop Sahak and the blessing of the king. It was also Mesrop who created a Georgian alphabet which was used to translate the Bible into Georgian. He also created an alphabet in Albanian which was used to translate the Bible in Albanian.

Between the sixth and eleventh centuries several thousand monasteries were founded in Europe. During this time, the orders of the Cistercians and Carthusians were founded. For a number of the monasteries, work meant working with books, where monks undertook the painstaking task of copying by hand the sacred texts of Christianity. As part of their work, the monks copied Bibles and Gospel books. They also copied biographies, histories, sermons, commentaries of the church fathers, and works of a secular nature. Nokter Labeo, a German monk and teacher at the monastic school of St. Gall in the tenth and eleventh centuries, translated both the *Psalter* and the *book of Job* by writing a section in Latin verse and then its German equivalent.

Other means of spreading Bible stories was through poetry, dramatic plays, and troubadours, who sang the Bible stories. By the 1100s certain religious groups were emerging who were encouraging the public to read. The Bible was also spread through traveling passion plays, poets, and the Scriptures themselves. The *Beghards* and *Beguines* in the Low Countries and the *Waldenses* in France were also demanding the vernacular languages for the people.

From Rome through Europe

However, a council of bishops met in Toulouse, France in 1229 to discuss the heretical activities of a group called the *Albigenses* and forbade anyone who was not a member of the clergy to own a Bible in any language.[9] In spite of this, Bibles in the languages of the people continued to appear. King Louis IX commissioned a complete Bible written in French. The translation of the Hebrew Bible into Spanish was undertaken by a rabbi under the supervision of a Benedictine monk and a Franciscan monk. Alfonso III ordered the translation of the Bible in Catalan.

In an effort to convert England's rulers to Christianity, in 597, Pope Gregory sent a Roman prior named Augustine to England along with forty monks, carrying a supply of books most likely from the pope's own library. This so impressed the king that he was converted to Christianity and, subsequently, was baptized. This opened the door for Augustine, the first bishop of Canterbury, to convert thousands of Jutes, Angles, and Saxons. At the same time, Irish monks came to England from an island in the Northwest, Iona.

Columba, a sixth century monk, was dedicated to copying the Scriptures. He may have copied the *Psalter*. Columba's name means "dove." He was born in 521 in Garton, Donegal into a princely family. He studied under some of the best scholars and developed a great love for the Scriptures. When Columba learned that his former master, Finnian, had the first copy of Jerome's *Book of Psalms* that had reached Ireland, he copied it against Finnian's wishes. When Finnian ordered him to return the book and the copy, he refused and the two went to King Diarmaid, who sided with Finnian.

Later when the king ordered that someone under Columba's protection be killed, the monk's clan attacked the king's forces. Three thousand men were killed. As a consequence, Columba was exiled. For his penance, he resolved to save at least three thousand souls to compensate for those lost in battle.

Through the centuries the Scriptures were copied and re-copied in the monasteries, not without errors, but nevertheless the Bible remained alive and was eventually put in the languages of the people.

9. Huber, *Bible through the Ages*, 239.

Missionary Monks

Missionaries

From the biblical days of Paul, Silas, Timothy, Barnabas, Mark, and nameless others, the impulse of the Christian movement was "to go." In spite of there being no Bible, with little or no formal church structure, with no "mission sending agencies," the gospel was almost immediately available to the furthest corners of the empire—and beyond. The mandate of Jesus in *Matthew's Gospel* and in Luke's *book of Acts* to "as you go preach the Gospel and teach all nations to observe all things" was from the first the rallying cry of the Christian movement.

While Paul was the first "missionary" mentioned in the *book of Acts*, there were already Christian communities in Antioch, Northern Africa, Rome, and Spain.

Early church history is full of Christians who went to other countries, taking the gospel with them. If there was no Bible in the language of the people, they would translate. If there were no literate languages, they would create an alphabet and then translate the Bible into that language.

Much of the missionary work of later centuries was actually carried out by the monks. The following list of missionaries and evangelists in the early church demonstrates the explosive spirit of the Christian movement.

FIG. 3: A TIMELINE OF CHRISTIAN EXPANSION

Year AD	Activity or Region Where the Gospel was Known
100	Christian Communities in Monaco, Algeria, and Sri Lanka.
117	Hadrian executes thousands of soldiers who had converted.
156	King Lucius of Great Britain wrote the bishop of Rome requesting to become a Christian.
174	First Christians reported in Austria.
196	Christians reported in Persia.
208	Christians reported on the far side of Hadrian's wall in Great Britain.
333	The king of Ethiopia makes Christianity the official religion of that country.
422	Patrick was in Ireland, having come from Britain as a kidnapped youth.
425	The first bishop in Afghanistan and Uzbekistan.
496	The conversion of Clovis, king of the Franks to orthodoxy.
500	Nimian, a Welchman, brought Christianity to the Picts of Scotland.
521	Columba also works with Picts in Scotland.
597	Pope sends Augustine and forty monks to England who set up a monastery and baptize King Aethelbert, who translates portions of Old Testament.
635	First missionaries in history travel to China.
625	King Edwin, non-Christian, of Northumbria asked to marry Ethelburga of Kent, a Christian. Edwin and his nobles were baptized on Easter 637, after a debate between Paulinus and the Druid high priest, Coifi. The priest was converted.
697	The Muslim invasion of Christian lands begins with the Muslim invasion of Carthage.
711	The Muslim invasion of Spain; the Moors remain in control of Spain until 1492.
717–41	Charles Martel, son of Pippin, king of Franks, stopped the Muslim advance in France in the great Battle of Tours in 732. He initiated a great missionary effort to convert western Germany.

680–754	*Boniface* was named a missionary bishop in Germany and organized the church in Bavaria and Thuringia. He founded the great Benedictine monastery of Fulda which became a center of priestly education and learning in Western Europe.
772–804	Charlemagne's power remained one of the greatest in middle Europe. In addition to his political power in uniting France and Germany, his conquest of the Saxons was important for the spread of Christianity.[10] By planting a series of bishoprics and monasteries throughout the Saxon land, he succeeded in converting the last Saxon tribe.
800s	King Alfred the Great translates Acts, Psalms, Exodus into Old English (Saxon).
1066	William the Conqueror, a Norman, defeated an English army at the Battle of Hastings. (See note below.) The introduction of the Norman language, a variation of French based on Latin, was introduced throughout England. *This marks the real beginning of the English language.*
1017	Danish King converts to Christianity.
1300s	Several important mission endeavors to China.
1600s	William Carey launched modern missions to India; Ignatius Loyola launched modern missions in the Catholic Church.

SUMMARY

For nearly one thousand years the Christian movement spread across the world—from China and India to the British Isles. Primarily due to two methods which often operated separately, but which eventually combined into a great endeavor of conversion, scholasticism, and education. The missionary/monastic movements overcame the paganism that existed in all of Europe and Great Britain.

---

10. Walker, *History of Christian*, 188–89.

CHAPTER 9 STUDY GUIDE

The decline of the Roman Empire is usually thought to start with the death of _____ in the year _____.

By the beginning of the third century, the church was making advances in _____, _____, and _____, and as far as _____.

All of this was being accomplished without _____.

Because of this lack, controversies regarding _____ were tearing the church apart. Some taught that Jesus was _____, others that he was _____, and yet others that _____.

With Constantine as emperor, _____ ended.

Before Constantine, _____ was the mark of the perfectly spiritual Christian.

Now, persons desiring spiritual perfection _____ _____.

The founder of Christian monasticism was _____ in the country of _____. He was born about _____.

He was impressed with the story of Jesus found in Matthew 19:2, in which Jesus told the rich, young man _____.

At first, monasticism was a _____ movement.

Initially, the solitary tradition grew into _____. This led to a _____ style of life, as seen in the early church in Luke's *book of Acts*.

As the church's clergy became more secular and worship became more formal, more and more such communities developed. The most influential order in the Western Church was that of _____. This became the founding example of monasticism.

Other strong monastic communities developed, among the first were the _____, started by a Benedictine monk named _____.

This order combined prayer, _____, and _____. A simple _____ and vows of _____ were their life.

Other movements were started by _____ of Assisi in Italy. They practiced begging for their food and supplies, peace-making, and the life of poverty.

Another order was started by _____, a native of Spain. Eventually, the Dominicans became the "_____" and provided leadership for _____.

The monasteries became the place where _____.

In the early fifth century, a monk known as Mesrop translated the Bible into _____, _____, and _____, after first developing an alphabet for these non-literate languages.

Between the sixth and eleventh centuries, _____ were founded in Europe.

As part of their work, the monks _____ and _____. They also copied _____, _____, and _____.

The Bible was also spread by means of _____, _____, and _____.

By the 1200s, groups were emerging who encouraged the public reading of the Scriptures. Chief among these were the _____ of France and Northern Italy.

However, in 1229, a group of bishops in Toulouse, France forbade _____.

In spite of this, _____ of France commissioned a complete Bible to be translated into French.

In an effort to convert Great Britain's rulers, Pope Gregory sent _____ in the year 597.

The result was _____ and his baptism.

This opened the door to present Christianity to the _____, which resulted in the conversion of thousands of _____, _____, and _____.

At the same time, _____ monks came to England from an island in the Northwest, the island of _____.

The most important of these monks was _____. He opened work in Scotland among the Picts. He also translated the *Psalms*.

The missionary movement began almost immediately after Christ's death. The first missionary mentioned in the *book of Acts* was _____.

But there were already Christian communities in _____, _____, _____, and _____.

Initially, as Christians moved throughout the empire, they took the message of Jesus with them, establishing churches and communities of believers. Much of the missionary work of later centuries was carried out by _____.

10

Beginnings of the English Language

THE DEVELOPMENT OF THE ENGLISH LANGUAGE

Have you ever tried to read *Beowulf, Canterbury Tales, Paradise Lost,* or an unabridged *King James Version of the Bible?* All are in English, but English at various stages of its development. Scholars divide the history of the English language into three periods.

1. Old English: from about 450–1200
2. Middle English: from 1200–1500
   a. Early: 1200–1300
   b. Late: 1300–1400
   c. Transitional to Modern English: 1400–1500
3. Modern English: from 1500–present

Anglo-Saxon was the form of Old English. When modern English emerged, the Midlands continued to speak the Mercian dialect, the language of Chaucer and Wycliffe (or Wycliff).

The most basic language in the British Isles was the *Celtic language*, which remains today as the language of Ireland and, to a great degree, that of Scotland. Other influences in forming the

BEGINNINGS OF THE ENGLISH LANGUAGE

English language came from the Romans, who brought Latin to the Islands and was the official legal and religious language for many centuries. A major development of the English language occurred when William the Conqueror defeated Harold at the Battle of Hastings in 1066. With the Normans came the French influence along with a resurgence of Latin. This mixture, with the Anglo-Saxon, provided the main ingredients of what became the English language.

The Norman Conquest in 1066 discouraged further translations. With the Normans came the use of French in much of the speech in Britain. The Normans spoke Anglo-Norman, a variation of Old French, which like other Romance languages continues Latin in another guise. French (Anglo-Norman) continued to be spoken by the elite. The masses of farmers continued to speak Anglo-Saxon.

Anglo-Saxon continued to be used and emerged in the fourteenth century with political changes bringing about a national unity and consciousness. Literary activity increased with such works as Chaucer and others. The language was now less confused with local dialects.[1]

In summary, the ordinary Englishman heard Latin in church, Anglo-Norman (French) in the law courts, and Anglo-Saxon in the streets.[2]

CHRISTIANITY COMES TO BRITAIN

Legend has it that Joseph of Arimathea brought Christianity to Britain, but there is no evidence to support this. Bede, the eighth century church historian, claims that Christianity reached Britain in 156, when Lucius, a British king, wrote the bishop of Rome "asking to become a Christian."

In sharp contrast to the stable and moderating ideals of Benedictine monasticism stands the Celtic type with its mystical

---

1. Wikgren, "English Bible," 85.
2. Kerr, *Ancient Texts*, 22.

spirit, its undisciplined restlessness, and its aesthetic rigor. The Celts arrived originally from the East by way of South Gaul; the Celtic language flourished from the fifth to the seventh centuries in Ireland, Scotland, and England—its unique contributions lying in its fervent missionary activity and its devotion to learning. Eventually, with the triumph of Roman Christianity in Britain, the Celtic monastery yielded to the Benedictine rule, but it infused its missionary spirit into later British monks like Willibrord and Boniface.[3] By the fourth century, the British were sending missionaries and evangelists to convert their neighbors. *Nithian*, a Welshman, brought the Bible to the Picts in Scotland.[4] England did not accept Christianity without problems. In 633, the pagan king Penda of Mercia slew the Christian King Edwin, and a heathen reaction followed in Northumbria. After a series of battles between Christian and non-Christian kings, Christianity was firmly established in Northumbria by 651.

The Venerable Bede

3. Walker et al., *History of Christian*, 128.
4. Huber, *Bible through the Ages*, 242.

BEGINNINGS OF THE ENGLISH LANGUAGE

Since the beginning, there had been controversy between the Roman missionaries and their Irish, or Old British, fellow Christians over structure and organization. Roman Christianity was firmly organized and diocesan, while the Old British church was monastic and tribal.[5] The two streams of missionary effort combined to the advantage of English Christianity. The Romans contributed order while the Old British gave missionary zeal and love of learning.[6] But significant advance began again with the missionaries sent out by Pope Gregory in 597 AD, and Christianity became firmly established.[7]

THE BIBLE IN GREAT BRITAIN

The story of the English Bible begins with the introduction of Christianity into Britain. The exact dates of when and how that happened are obscure, but in the early third century Tertullian and Origen are witnesses to the existence of British Christianity, the former stating that there were places in Britain subject to Christ which Roman arms could not penetrate.[8]

The Bible played a central part in English Christianity. The Bible which was used in the earliest English Church, as in the British and Irish churches, was the Latin Bible. In no part of the Western world was the version studied more diligently and copied more lovingly and faithfully than in Great Britain and Ireland. It was copied under the direction of *Abbot Ceolfrid* in one or the other of two monasteries: Jarrow or Wearmouth.[9]

The first name that comes to us when thinking of straightforward translation of the Bible is that of Aldhelm, first Bishop of Sherborne, in Dorset. He is said to have translated the *Psalter* just after 700. But there was a man in England whose reputation

---

5. Huber, *Bible through the Ages*, 242.
6. Huber, *Bible through the Ages*, 242.
7. Huber, *Bible through the Ages*, 242.
8. Wikgren, "English Bible," 84.
9. Bruce, *English Bible*, 1.

for learning throughout Western Europe was even greater than Aldhelm's. This was *Bede,* the monk of Jarrow. His concern for his less learned fellow countrymen led him to give them parts of the New Testament in their own language. During his last illness he was busy translating the Gospel of John and got as far as "What are these among so man" (John 6:9). Bede died on the Ascension eve (May 25) in 735.[10]

The English king, *Alfred the Great,* was a learned man interested in literature and culture and the promotion of good among his subjects. He translated into English: Bede's *Ecclesiastical History of the English Nation,* Orosius' *Universal History*, Pope Gregory the Great's *Pastoral Care,* and portions of *Exodus.*

A complete translation of the Bible is unknown in this Anglo-Saxon period. A Bible for the layman was also unthinkable in the medieval church, which saw in the wide use of the Bible a threat to unity and ecclesiastical control over the interpretation of Scripture, as well as a profanation of the Scriptures through such rough dialects as Anglo-Saxon.[11] However, Anglo-Saxon Christianity was to produce some of the most energetic of missionaries by whom the gospel and papal obedience were alike to be advanced on the continent.[12]

In sermon and minstrel song, the Scriptures first became known in the earliest English form, that is, Anglo-Saxon. Soon, partial translations were put into written form. A complete translation, however, is unknown in this Anglo-Saxon period.

Caedmon, a seventh century cowherd of Northern England, in an overnight vision, was commissioned to sing verses of the Bible in Anglo-Saxon as it was read to him. In Southern England, at the same time (about 700 AD), *Abbott Aldhelm* used the minstrel technique to present Bible stories to large numbers.[13]

While the Bible itself was not available to the common man, other means of communicating the gospel were being developed.

10. Bruce, *English Bible*, 6.
11. Wikgren, "English Bible," 84.
12. Walker et al., *History of Christian*, 182.
13. Kerr, *Ancient Texts*, 23.

Beginnings of the English Language

The stained-glass windows of the churches told the Bible stories. Traveling thespian groups staged dramatic presentation in public places telling Bible stories. Troubadours with Bible songs traveled from town to town singing the Gospel stories.[14]

The cycles of miracle plays dealt with twenty-one Old Testament episodes and sixty-eight episodes from the New Testament. Written in Middle English, these plays reached the height of popularity in the late fourteenth and fifteenth centuries.

The Venerable Bede is supposed to have translated the Lord's Prayer and the Apostles' Creed for the benefit of priests. He is also credited with translating the Gospels.

Other attempts at translating the Bible were:

- Seventh century translations by Aldhelm, bishop of Sherborne, translated the Psalms into Anglo-Saxon. He died in 709.
- Egbert, bishop of holy island (Lindisfarne), translated the Gospels.
- Ninth century Vespasian Psalter in Old English remains today.
- Tenth century Alfred the Great translated various portions of the Bible, as mentioned previously.
- The West-Saxon Gospels give a full and readable translation that comes close to modern standards. The date is uncertain and the translator is unknown.
- Bishop Leofric presented a translation to Exeter Cathedral in 1072.
- Aaelfric, the Grammarian (955–1020), wrote the *Heptateuch,* a free English paraphrase of the first seven books of the Bible.

> Luke's version of the Lord's Prayer, from Lindisfarne Monastery, Ireland, around 700.[15] *Fader gehaldad sie nōma tōcymae ric in hiaf useme daeghuaemlice sel us*

---

14. Kerr, *Ancient Texts*, 32.
15. The five Old English texts are from Kerr, *Ancient Texts.*

> *eghuele daege ſ [f]get us synna usra gif faeslice aec þe [f] gfaes eghuelc scyldge us [f]get ne usic ōnlaedu in costunge*

The parable of the sower (Matt 13:3–5) from the Wessex Gospels, ca. 900.

> *Sothlice ut code se sawere his saed to sawenne, And tha tha he scow, sumu hie feollon with weg, and fuglas common and aeton tha. Sotthlice sum feollon on staenihte, thaer hit naefde micle corthan, and hraedlice up stungon, for thaem the hie naefdon thaere eorthaan diepaan; sotlice, up sprungenre sunnan, hie adruggodon and forscruncon, for thaem the hie naefdon wyrtruman.*

Wyclif's version of the Lord's Prayer, 1380s:

> *Fadir, that art in heunene, halewid be thi name. Thi kingdom come to. {Z}yue to vs, thi wille be don, as in heunene, and in erthe. Oure eche days breed uyeue us to day. And for[z]yue to va oure dettys, as and we for[z]yuers oure dettourys. And ne leed not vs in to temptacioun but deleuere us of yuel. Amen.* (Matt 6:9–13)

Tyndale's translation of the Lord's Prayer, ca. 1535:

> *Our Father which art in hév, hallowed be thy name. Lett thy kyngdom come. Thy will, be fulfilled, even in erth as it is in heven. Oure dayly breed geve vs this daye. And forgeve vs oure sysnnes for even we forgeve every man that traspaseth vs, and ledde vs not into temptaci, Butt deliver vs from evyll. Amen.*

The original translation of the Twenty-Third Psalm in the Authorized (King James) Version, 1611:

> *The Lord is my shepherd, I shall not want. He maketh me to lie downe in greene pastures; he leadeth mee beside the still waters. He restoreth mey soule: he leadeth me in the pathes of righteousness, for his names sake. Yea, though I walke through the valley of the shadowe of death, I will feare no euill: for thou art with me, thy rod and they staff, the comfort me. Thou preparest a table before me in the presence of mine enemies; thou annointest me head with*

oyle, my cuppe runneth ouer Surely goodness and mercy shall followe me all the days of my life, and I will dwell in the house of the Lord for euer.

The people were hungry for the gospel in whatever form it was presented. The people were ready to have the Bible in their own language.[16]

---

16. Related recommended reading for this chapter: Peters, *Brother Cadfael Chronicles*. Cadfael is a monk in the Benedictine Abbey of Saint Peter and Saint Paul of Shrewsbury. The setting is 1145 CE. There is always a mystery to solve.

CHAPTER 10 STUDY GUIDE

The English language—as with all languages—is constantly developing. Old English took shape around _____.

Modern English, as we might recognize it, took form around _____.

Old English was actually _____ _____.

The oldest or most basic language in the British Isles was _____.

_____ was the official legal and religious language for many centuries.

In _____ William the Conqueror defeated Harold at _____.

This conquest brought the _____ language to Britain.

The common Englander continued to use _____ in church, but he used _____ in everyday life.

Legend says that _____ brought Christianity to Britain.

Two types of monastic groups were in Britain, the _____ and the _____.

Nithian, a Welchman, brought the Bible to the _____.

The first person who translated any part of the Bible into Anglo-Saxon was _____, first bishop of Sherborne.

The greatest learned man in Western Europe was the monk _____.

A _____ was unthinkable in the medieval church.

Different ways of presenting the Bible other than reading were: _____, _____, and _____.

In the Roman Church the Bible remained in the _____ language until the 1950s.

11

The Development of the English Language

So far as we know, the first complete English Bible was due to the influence and activity of John Wycliffe (1324/1328–1384), the able and eloquent Oxford scholar who was called "the morning star of the Reformation," because of the religious convictions he developed and propagated. Wycliffe was, in addition to being a scholar, a teacher, priest, and theologian.[1] In common with later Protestantism, he emphasized the necessity of the layman to have the opportunity of reading the Bible. Since he was also active in efforts for social justice, his appeal was widespread among the common people.

John Wycliffe was born in Hipswell in Yorkshire. He entered Balliol College, Oxford of which, for a short time, and he became "master." In Oxford he rose to great scholarly distinction, lecturing to large classes and was esteemed the ablest theologian on the faculty. He was deeply influenced by Augustine and through Augustine by Platonic concepts. Wycliffe gradually became known outside of Oxford.[2]

---

1. Norwood, *Development*, 31.
2. Walker et al., *History of Christian*, 628.

By 1376, it was the wealth of the church and clerical interference, especially that of the popes in political life that aroused his opposition. In 1377, Pope Gregory XI issued five "bulls" ordering Wycliffe's arrest and examination. Yet, Wycliffe enjoyed the protection of a strong party at court and much popular support.[3] Wycliffe was now developing his reforming activities with many writings in English and Latin. What he was coming to believe and to proclaim were:

1. The Scriptures are the only law of the church.
2. The church itself is not centered in the pope and cardinals.
3. The church is centered in the whole of the elect; its head is Jesus Christ.
4. Since the pope might not be one of the elects, Wycliffe did not reject the papacy as such.
5. A pope who grasps worldly power and is eager for taxes is presumptively non-elect.[4]

The Wycliffe translation was very popular and many copies survive up to today. Some of its diction and literary style, and much of its spirit, lives on in the mainstream of subsequent translation and revision.

He was now fighting current churchly conditions all along the line. In 1383–1384 he made English translations from the Latin Vulgate, against the express position of the church officials, who were opposed to putting the Bible into the hands of common people. The church's fear was that this might corrupt them,[5] but what really raised the hostility of the church against him was his questioning the doctrine of *transubstantiation*, which made of every mass a miracle.

Transubstantiation is the doctrine that the bread and wine of the mass actually become the body and blood of Christ through certain words that the priest speaks. Wycliffe spoke of the "idolatry of the priests of Baal, who worship gods they have

---

3. Walker et al., *History of Christian*, 269.
4. Walker et al., *History of Christian*, 269.
5. Wikgren, "English Bible," 86.

The Development of the English Language

Wycliffe Sends His Lollards

made." Also, the presumptuous belief that the church could grant to "sinners the power to make God."[6]

After his forced retirement to Lutterworth in 1382, and his death in 1384, his followers, "the poor priests" or "Lollards," carried on his work in an influential traveling ministry of teaching, preaching, and distribution of the Scriptures.

Wycliffe managed to survive the attack of his enemies and to die a natural death. However, his writings were banned, and in 1415 the Council of Constance officially ordered his body and all his works to be burned. The cause of religion was thus advanced by the digging up and burning of his bones in 1428, the ashes being thrown into the River Swift. The disposal of Wycliffe's remains was symbolic, however, of real religious progress through the spread of the Scriptures which he brought about. The Wycliffe Bible has been described as "an event rather than merely a book," both on this account and because of its effect upon sixteenth century English prose style.[7] Wycliffe's part in the project is obscure. A pupil and colleague, Nicolas of Hereford, might have done most of the work, assisted perhaps by another friend, John Purvey. Purvey is also credited with the revision which occurred in 1388 and became the popular and standard form.

An edict of 1408, forbidding the unauthorized translation and publication in English or other language, discouraged the printing

---

6. Norwood, *Development*, 32.
7. Norwood, *Development*, 32.

of the Bible in the fifteenth century. The Wycliffe translation was very popular, and many copies survive up to today. Some of its diction and literary style—and much of its spirit—lives on in the mainstream of subsequent translation and revision. It remained the only English Bible until the sixteenth century. Wycliffe left no organized followers, but his influence is seen in two different directions:

- The *Lollards* of England continued going throughout the country, taking Wycliffe's Bible and preaching its message in the language of the people. This continued to the Reformation.
- The *Hussites* of Bohemia, who made use of Wycliffe's teachings and writings. John Huss was a priest and popular preacher and rector of the University of Prague. He is one of the most colorful and heroic figures in Bohemian history. Because he proclaimed the writings and teachings of Wycliffe, he was soon in deep trouble with the authorities.

John Hus
1369 - July 6, 1415

"Seek the truth
Listen to the truth
Teach the truth
Love the truth
Abide by the truth
And defend the truth
unto death."

When the pope ordered the archbishop of Prague to burn Wycliffe's books, Huss refused and preached a sermon on the theme: "for the Pope, I know not whether he be in heaven or hell, has written on his wretched parchments to the archbishop to burn the books of Master John Wycliffe, wherein are many good things."[8] In 1414, Huss was granted safe conduct to attend the Council of Constance, but was imprisoned upon arrival. He was executed by suffering torture, humiliation and degradation, and eventual burning at the stake. As with Wycliffe, his ashes were thrown into the river. The Hussites remain in existence today as the Moravian Church.

In 1528, Sir Thomas More, Lord Chancellor of England, published *A Dialogue Concerning Heresies* in which he launched "a fierce attack upon the English version of the New Testament lately completed by William Tyndale." In the course of his attack he refers to John Wycliffe as the "great arch-heretic Wycliffe," who undertook "of a malicious purpose" to translate the Bible into English and "purposely corrupted the holy text."[9] Yet it is held by some, that when the citizens of London welcomed the first Elizabeth as their queen in 1558 and presented her with "The Word of Truth," the volume which she so gratefully received was a copy of the Wycliffe Gospels. What a fitting climax to the history of the first English Bible.[10]

John Wycliffe

8. Norwood, *Development*, 32.
9. Bruce, *English Bible*, 22.
10. Bruce, *English Bible*, 23.

CHAPTER 11 STUDY GUIDE

John Wycliffe was a scholar teacher who was called
"_____."

In addition to being a scholar, he was also a _____
_____.

He strongly believed that laypeople _____.

He was a student and later a "master" of _____.

The church father _____ greatly influenced him.

Wycliffe's opposition to the church was caused by
_____ and _____.

By 1376, Wycliffe was developing other beliefs concerning the church:

1. _____
2. _____
3. _____
4. _____
5. _____

In 1383 he translated the English Bible from _____.

What really aroused him was the church's teaching about transubstantiation. What is this teaching? _____
_____.

He was also against the idea that _____.

In 1382, he was forced to retire to the village of _____, where he died in _____.

_____ carried on his work as traveling preachers.

The Council of Constance, in 1415, ordered _____
_____.

The Development of the English Language

The Wycliffe translation remained the only English Bible until _____.

His influence is seen in two different ways:
   The _____ who continued Wycliffe's message and translation up to the _____.

His teachings and translation was taken up by _____.
   His followers were called _____.

Hus refused to burn the works of Wycliffe when ordered by the pope and was subsequently _____ and _____.

The followers of John Hus eventually became _____.

In 1528, Sir Thomas More called Wycliffe "_____" who "_____."

Yet, in 1558, the Bible presented to the first Queen Elizabeth was _____.

12

William Tyndale, Miles Coverdale, and Others

With the sixteenth century we enter into the most creative period in the history of the English Bible. It was a time of bitter Protestant-Catholic conflict, of widespread ignorance of the Scriptures (even among the clergy), and of initial opposition to vernacular translations in England—both Catholic and Anglican alike. But forces were at work in the Renaissance and Reformation within a very few years that led to the legal dissemination of the Bible in English. The momentous discovery of printing took place. The Scriptures were made known in their original languages—the first Hebrew Bible appearing in 1418 and the first Greek New Testament, the edition of Erasmus, in 1516. Scholars like Erasmus, William Tyndale, and reformers like Luther spoke for and worked for the right of all people to read the sacred texts. These and other factors set the stage for the production of the first printed English Bible.

At this time, William Tyndale came upon the scene. (He sometimes used the alternative family name of Hutchins.) He was born about 1492–1495 and was educated at Oxford. but after a year he moved to Cambridge—which was more advanced than Oxford as a home of the new learning.[1] His experience as chaplain and tutor led him to the conviction that it was impossible to "*sablysh the laye people in any trurh, excepte the scripture were plainly lyde before their eyes in their mother tonge.*"[2] Tyndale was well-qualified both by an excellent knowledge of Greek and Hebrew and by an ability to write English so well that his graceful style has come to be immortalized in the English Bible.

William Tyndale

Another quality that Tyndale possessed was perseverance in the face of persecution and opposition. The clergy, supported by the government, were opposed to translation in general and specifically to Tyndale's growing Protestant views. Nor was he helped by his vigorous denunciation of the clergy. Neither was he able to find support from London's Bishop Tunstall. However, Tyndale did find support in a wealthy London cloth merchant, Humphrey Monmouth, in whose home Tyndale began his translation. At this

1. Bruce, *English Bible*, 28.
2. Pollard, *Records of the English Bible*; quoted in Wikgren, "English Bible," 86.

time, he became aware of the teachings of Luther and realized that he "vndersstode at the laste not only that there was no Crowne in my lorde of Londons palace to translate the new testament, but also there was no place to do it in all englende, as experience doth now openly declare."[3]

Therefore, Tyndale left for Hamburg, Germany, and by mid-1525, his New Testament was complete, and printing was begun at Cologne. Printing was interrupted by the authorities at the instigation of an enemy of the reformers, Johan Dobneck, where the printer, Peter Quentel, printed ten sheets before he was forbidden by the authorities to finish. It is believed that three thousand copies were printed, but only a thirty-one-page fragment of Matthew remains in the British Museum.[4]

Tyndale was urged to take his manuscripts to Worms, where the work was completed. The first completed printed English New Testament appeared toward the end of February 1526. Copies were beginning to reach England about a month later. So strong was the opposition to Tyndale's translations by the English king and bishops that they worked together to destroy Tyndale's translation as copies were smuggled into England. Of this "octavo edition" only two copies survive, other than a small fragment; one is in the Baptist College at Bristol, England, and the other is in the library of St. Paul's Cathedral, London.[5]

Tyndale was able to continue with the support of a number of London merchants, particularly Augustine Packynton, who raised money by selling Tyndale's New Testaments to the bishop of London for burning. Thus, keeping Tyndale and the Bishop's bonfire going.[6]

In October 1526, Bishop Cuthbert Tonstall took steps to gather up as many of Tyndale's copies as he could, ordering their owners to hand them over on pain of excommunication or worse, and then he burned them publically at St Paul's Cross.

3. Wikgren, "English Bible," 87.
4. Wikgren, "English Bible," 87.
5. Wikgren, "English Bible," 87.
6. Wikgren, "English Bible," 87.

Tyndale's association with Luther at Wittenberg and his indebtedness to Luther's German New Testament were more reasons for official condemnation. The authorities were also upset by Tyndale's substitution for certain ecclesiastical terms, such as: "elder" for "priest," "repentance" for "penance," and "congregation" for "church."

Tyndale's Execution by Fire

Tyndale revised his translation in 1534, and again in 1535. This latter translation became the basis for all later revisions. Tyndale also undertook a translation of the Old Testament but was unable to finish it before his death. He finished the *Pentateuch* in 1530 and *Jonah* in 1531.

The authorities apprehended him through the treachery of a friend, and after an imprisonment of a year and a half near Brussels, he was strangled and burned at the stake on October 6, 1536. According to Foxe (author of *Foxe's Book of Martyrs*), his dying words were "Lord, open the King of England's eyes."[7] But the

---

7. Kerr, *Ancient Texts*, 61.

political scene in England was already changing under Cromwell, who had sought Tyndale's release. A complete English Bible was now freely in circulation.

Tyndale's translation was the first English New Testament to be printed.[8] The invention of the printing press began a new era of learning and interest in the classics of Latin and Greek, and such English literature as Chaucer, and French classics. Another important event which contributed to the revival of learning was the Turkish capture of Constantinople in 1433. For eleven hundred years it had been the center of the Eastern Roman Empire and also the seat of the Orthodox Church. It was a center of Greek learning. With the capture of the city, many Greek scholars migrated to the West, bringing their manuscripts and learning with them. The study of the Greek New Testament received new importance.[9]

The creative nature of Tyndale's work cannot be overestimated. Though he freely consulted the Vulgate, Luther's New Testament, Erasmus' New Testament, and Wycliffe's English Bible, his work is characterized by great originality and vigor. In fact, it became the foundation for all subsequent revisions. Eighty percent of the English Bibles down through the Revised Standard Version is basically the parts of the Bible he translated.

Next to Tyndale, the man to whom lovers of the English Bible owe the greatest debt is Myles Coverdale (1488–1569). Coverdale was not the scholar that Tyndale was, but the best part of his life was making the Bible accessible to his fellow countrymen in their own language. The "Coverdale's Bible" appeared in 1535. He also edited the Great Bible of 1539 and had some part in the preparation of the Geneva Bible in 1560.

Myles Coverdale was a native of York, graduate of Cambridge, and an Augustinian friar. He left his orders after coming under the influence of the Reformation movement. In 1528 he sought refuge on the continent where he spent some time as an assistant to Tyndale in Hamburg, and as a proofreader in Antwerp. In 1535 he returned to England where he was under the patronage of

---

8. Bruce, *Engish Bible*, 25.
9. Bruce, *English Bible*, 26

Anne Boleyn and Thomas Cromwell. But with Anne's execution, Cromwell's fall from power, and a change in the king's ecclesiastical policy in 1540, Coverdale returned to the continent. After the accession of King Edward VI, he returned to England and became bishop of Exeter.

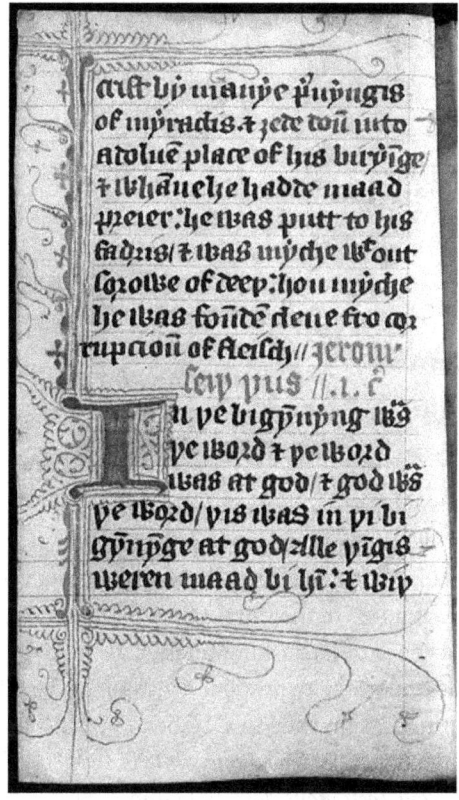

Gospel of John Chapter 1, Coverdale's Bible

When Mary, sister of Edward, ascended the throne, he was deposed, and it was only through the intervention of the king of Denmark that he did not go to the stake as did so many Reformers during her reign. Coverdale went to Geneva where he became an elder in the English Church and stood as godfather to the minister's second son. That minister was John Knox. Another tie with Scotland was Coverdale's wife, Elizabeth Macheson, a Scotswoman.

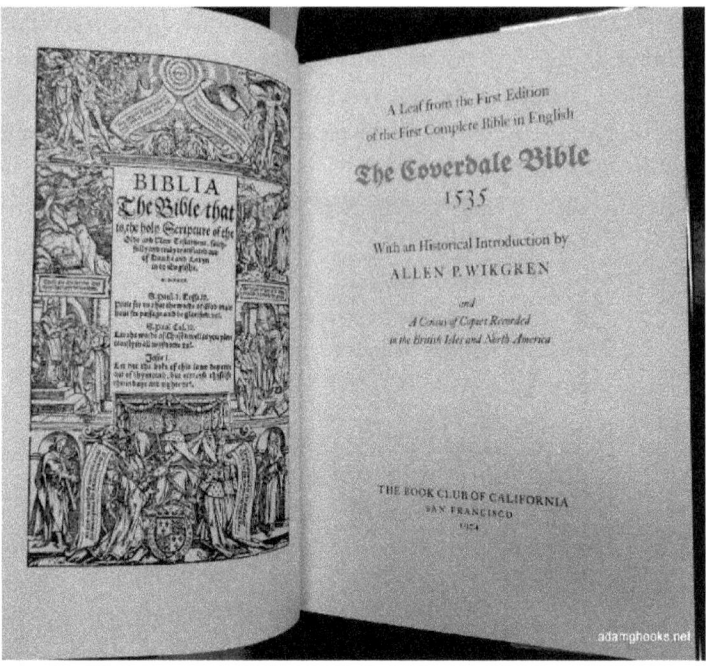

Coverdale returned to England the last time in 1515. For the last ten years of his life he did not participate much in public affairs. Between his failing health and his strong Puritan convictions, he did not feel at home in the Elizabethan religious atmosphere. It was at the insistence of Jacob van Meteren, an Antwerp merchant that Coverdale undertook to produce a version of the Bible in English. The printing was finished in October 1535 and the work was published under the title, *The Bible, that is the Holy Scripture of the Olde and New Testament, faithfully and truly translated out of Douche and Latyn into Englishe.* A dedication to King Henry VIII was in the introduction, for the king was more of a "defender of the faith" than the pope realized.[10]

---

10. Wikgren, "English Bible," 88. Both the Title and the Dedication are contained in this reference.

SUMMARY: COVERDALE'S BIBLE

- Coverdale's Bible was the first to introduce chapter summaries as distinct from the text.
- Coverdale's Bible was the first to separate the Apocrypha from the other Old Testament books.
- Because of Coverdale's Lutheran affinity there was some moderate and some very hostile opposition to this version by churchmen. With the death of Anne Boleyn, Coverdale's Bible fell into disfavor—although it was reprinted twice in 1537, once in 1550, and again in 1553.

CHAPTER 12 STUDY GUIDE

In England, the sixteenth century was a time of bitter _____ and _____ conflict.

There was widespread ignorance of Scriptures among _____.

The invention of _____ greatly helped distribute the Bible.

Luther worked for _____.

Tyndale's experience as chaplain and tutor led him to the conviction that _____.

In addition to his knowledge of languages and superb knowledge of English, his _____ led him to great popularity.

When the bishop of London would not help him, Tyndale _____ _____. In Worms, the work _____.

_____ was a wealthy London merchant who helped Tyndale.

The first completed printed English Bible appeared in _____.

Augustine Packynton helped sell Tyndale's Bible by _____ _____.

In October 1526, Bishop Tonstall _____ _____.

The authorities were upset with Tyndale's substitution of several words in his New Testament such as:

_____ for _____

_____ for _____

William Tyndale, Miles Coverdale, and Others

_____ for _____

In 1535, while living in Antwerp, Belgium, in a free city, Tyndale was kidnapped, taken to Belguim outside of Antwerp and _____, _____, and finally, _____.

Tyndale's last words while burning at the stake were _____ _____.

Myles Coverdale was a graduate of Cambridge and was also _____.

He left his _____ after coming under the influence of the _____ movement.

He worked as assistant to _____ in Hamburg, and as a _____ in Antwerp.

In England he was sponsored by _____ and _____.

When Edward VI was king, Coverdale became _____.

With Mary, Queen of Scots as queen, his life was saved by intervention from _____.

Back in Geneva, he was godfather to the second son of _____.

Coverdale returned to England in 1515 and spent his last ten years _____.

The Coverdale Bible is _____.

The Bible was dedicated to _____.

13

The First Completed Printed English Bible

With the groundwork of Wycliffe and Tyndale and others, plus the recent invention of the printing press, the number of printed Bible translations increased greatly. Some were produced by competent, careful translators while others were hurried works by copiers and clerks.

The Lollard movement survived Wycliffe's death and so did the persecution. Some of Wycliffe's followers were burned at the stake. Parliament passed anti-Lollard legislation. Despite the ban, the Lollard movement and the reading of the English Scripture continued until the reign of Henry V (1413–1422), who took vigorous measures against the Lollards. Persecutions and burnings continued but could not stop the Lollard movement. In 1408, Archbishop Arundel prepared a constitution which the Provincial Council at Oxford adopted. It declared in part:

> The Holy Scripture is not to be translated into the vulgar tongue, nor a translation to be expounded, until it shall have been duly examined, under pain of excommunication and the stigma of heresy . . . those who read the Scripture in their mother tongue without

authorization would forfeit land, cattle, life and goods from their heirs forever.[1]

William Tyndale would be the first to combine the new learning and the new technology to produce vernacular Scriptures.

The change that swept Europe during Wycliffe's and Tyndale's times was the *Renaissance,* meaning "the new birth." A host of previously unknown manuscripts were found and Italian scholars set themselves to studying and collating these exciting new texts. A new interest in "truth" emerged. It was no longer good enough to ask, "Who said it?" but now the urgency of the times required that one ask, "What was being taught?"

By the beginning of the sixteenth century, England had changed a great deal. After thirty years of dynastic conflict in the "War of the Roses" (1455–1485), between the House of York and the House of Tudor, the Tudors, the last being Elizabeth I, transformed England by instituting the first truly national, centralized, and efficient government. The general population ceased to look upon the established church as a source of spirituality.[2]

At Oxford, John Colet, son of the Mayor of London, whose influential friends kept him from execution,[3] began to lecture directly from the plain Scripture rather than complicated interpretations followed by medieval scholastics. He was followed by George Stafford. At Cambridge, Erasmus, the brightest light of new learning, visited these universities and was included in the intimate circle surrounding Henry VIII. These "Oxford Reformers" were attacked by the monks and friars who still dominated the universities. Colet later became Dean of St. Paul's Cathedral in London and established a school along "modern" lines with an emphasis on Greek, Latin, and the classics.[4]

Erasmus confessed in 1516, that he longed for the day when common people could read the Bible, that "the husbandman may

---

1. Kerr, *Ancient Texts,* 39.
2. Kerr, *Ancient Texts,* 46.
3. See "John Colet."
4. Bruce, *English Bible,* 26.

sing parts of the Gospel at his plow, that the weaver may warble them at his shuttle."[5]

MATTHEW'S BIBLE

In 1537, there appeared a folio volume with the title, "*The Byble, which is all the holy Scripture: In which are contayned the Olde and Newe Testament, truly and purely translated into Englysh by Thomas Matthew.*" Thomas Matthew was the pen name for John Rogers, a former associate of Tyndale's, who later was the first martyr of Queen Mary.[6] This Bible was probably printed in Antwerp.[7] Very important are the words at the bottom of the title page, namely, "Set forth with the kings [sic] most gracious lycence."

Due to the influence of Archbishop Cranmer on Thomas Cromwell to obtain the royal license for this new version, the royal license was granted, thus assuring that anyone could read this Bible without danger of persecution. This license was also granted to *Coverdale's Bible*. So now, there were two "authorized" versions of the Bible afloat in England: *Matthew's Bible,* which was essentially Tyndale's *Pentateuch* and the historical books as far as *2 Chronicles*, and Coverdale's translation of the other Old Testament books and the Apocrypha and Tyndale's New Testament of 1535. It was ironic that the first English Bible to be published under royal license was essentially Tyndale's Bible, although it was not yet wise to publish under Tyndale's name.[8]

By now the clergy were encouraged to possess a copy of the English Bible for themselves. Some bishops went so far as to require that by Whitsunday 1538, an English Bible be chained to the pulpit so that "literate parishioners should read and illiterate parishioners might listen."[9]

5. Bruce, *English Bible*, 26.
6. Bruce, *English Bible*, 64.
7. Huber, *Bible through the Ages*, 310.
8. Huber, *Bible through the Ages*, 65.
9. Bruce, *English Bible*, 92.

The First Completed Printed English Bible

But because of the evident "Protestantisms" in the marginal notes, it was not supported by the more conservative bishops and clergy, it was decided that a revision of the *Matthew Bible* be revised. The revision was given to Coverdale and the printing began in Paris in May 1538. This was the beginning of what was to become known as *The Great Bible*.[10] In 1538, an injunction in the king's name went out to the clergy that the *largest* copy of an English Bible be conveniently placed in every church so that persons might conveniently read, discuss, and be bound to follow, etc., the next Feast of All Saints.

Evidently Cromwell had in mind the *Great Bible* because of its size. But because the *Great Bible* would not be available by November, many clergy were perplexed because they wanted to be obedient to the king's mandate. So they resorted to purchasing the *Coverdale Bible* because it was the largest sized Bible in England. The *Coverdale Bible* was so popular that parishioners were reading it even during worship, to the extent that the king issued a proclamation (towards the end of April 1539) forbidding the reading of the English Bible out loud in church during divine service.[11]

The printing of the *Great Bible* was further delayed by the French Inquisitor General at the end of 1538. He forbade printing to continue and confiscated copies already printed. Diplomatic pressures caused him to allow the transport of the printing presses and other equipment to be shipped to England where printing could continue. However, the confiscated copies were not released. Thus, the Great Bible made its first appearance in April 1539.

THE TAVERNER BIBLE

Shortly before the *Great Bible* was published, another revision of *Matthew's Bible* was published in England by a layman scholar,

---

10. Bruce, *English Bible*, 67.
11. Huber, *Bible through the Ages*, 311; see also 68–69.

Richard Taverner. It had little influence because it was immediately overshadowed by the *Great Bible*.[12]

THE GREAT BIBLE

The *Great Bible* of 1539 bears the title:[13]

> *The Byble in Englyshe, that is to saye the content of all the holy scripture, both of the olde and newe testament, truly translated after the veryte of the Hebrew and Greke texts, by the dylygent study of dyurse excellent learned men, expert in the forsayde tonges. Prynted by Richard Grafton and Edward Whitchurch. Cum riulegio ad imprimendum solum. 1539.*

The Great Bible was actually Coverdale's revision of John Roger's revision of Tyndale's Bible. Coverdale was not content with the first edition and so he continued working on it and published a second version of the Great Bible in 1540. It was superior to the first edition, especially in the poetical section of the Old and New Testament.

One ironic fact is that this Bible was mandated by "right reverend fathers in God" Cuthbert, bishop of Durham and Nicolas, bishop of Rochester. Yes, that's right! The same Bishop Cuthbert who is Cuthbert Tunstall, formerly bishop of London, who bought up as many copies of Tyndale's Bibles to burn them at St. Paul's Cross. Bishop Tunstall knew that he was authorizing a Bible that relied heavily on Tyndale's translations, yet under King Henry's command he was forced to sanction works that he had once tried so hard to abolish.[14]

Around 1541 a reaction to so many English language Bibles set in. There was a Catholic reaction which halted the publication of the Bible. Bibles were burned, and both Protestants and Catholics were burned for heresy. In 1543 restrictions were placed

---

12. Bruce, *English Bible*, 69.
13. Wikgren, "English Bible," 90n13. Bruce, *English Bible*, 92.
14. Huber, *Bible through the Ages*, 310–11.

on the reading of the Bible. The Great Bible was the only version allowed; all other versions were burned in 1543. When Catholic Mary Tudor (also known as "Bloody Mary") ascended to the throne, a severe Catholic persecution took place in which more than three hundred martyrs occurred, including Cranmer. Many, such as Coverdale, took refuge in Geneva, Switzerland and found a sympathetic group of people.

THE GENEVA BIBLE

In the previous chapter, we referred to the situation in which Coverdale fled to Geneva during the purges of Queen Mary Tudor. While there, Coverdale, John Calvin, John Knox, and Beza worked together to produce the *Geneva Bible*. This was primarily a revision of previous translations.

The first edition of the complete Geneva Bible is sometimes called the *Breeches Bible*, because of the translation of Genesis 3:7; it states that Adam and Eve "sewed figge-tree leaves together and made themselves breeches." A new translation of the *Geneva Bible* was the most scholarly and accurate English Bible produced so far. Roman type was used for the first time. Division of chapters into verses was first used. Due to these features, the *Geneva Bible* immediately became very popular. It soon became the household Bible of English-speaking Protestants and remained so for more than a century.[15]

The *Geneva Bible* was the Bible of Shakespeare, of the Puritan Pilgrims who brought this Bible to America, and of King James I himself.[16]

THE BISHOP'S BIBLE

The *Geneva Bible* was disliked by the clergy and government. Also, the *Great Bible* was losing its appeal. So, there was an attempt for a

15. Wikgren, "English Bible," 92.
16. "Geneva," paras. 2–3.

revision. In 1564, Archbishop Parker formed a committee of revisers who produced a revision satisfactory to the Church of England and the clergy. Since the majority of the committee were Bishops, the revision was called the *Bishop's Bible*.[17]

In spite of many defects, the *Bishop's Bible* became the second "authorized" Bible, although it was never so designated by the queen. It was endorsed by a convocation in 1571 that ordered its possession and use by every bishop and archbishop. This version eventually displaced the *Great Bible* as the one to be read in churches. The Psalter of the *Great Bible* was retained.

BIBLE BLOOPERS

The Coverdale Bible is nicknamed the "Bug Bible" because it advises, "Thou shalt not need to be afrayed for eny bugges by night" (Ps 91:5).

The *Murderer's Bible* misprints "murderers" for "murmurers" (Jude 1:6).

The *Printer's Bible*, an edition of the King James Version, laments that "printers" not "princes" have persecuted me without cause" (Ps 119:161).

The *Wife-hater Bible* warns of the consequences "if any man come to me, and hate not his father . . . and his own wife also. . ." instead of his own "life" (Luke 24:6).

The *Adulterer's Bible* leaves out an essential "not," and commands, "thou shalt commit adultery" (Exod 20:14).

The *Bishop's Bible* was the Bible of the Church of England and went through twenty editions in forty-two years serving as the official basis for the King James Version, which took from it a number of well-known phrases.

---

17. Wikgren, "English Bible," 92.

The First Completed Printed English Bible

CHAPTER 13 STUDY GUIDE

The invention of the printing press caused _____.

Some translations were by _____, yet others were by _____.

The _____ survived Wycliffe's death for more than _____.

Some of Wycliffe's followers _____.

King _____ took vigorous measures against Wycliffe's followers.

In 1408, Archbishop Arundel had a council that declared _____ _____.

The movement of change during Wycliffe's and Tyndale's time was called the _____, which means _____.

The War of the Roses was between _____.

The general population lost faith in _____.

_____ was called the "brightest light of new learning."

Thomas Matthew was the pen name for _____, who had worked with _____ in Bible translating.

His Bible was called _____.

The Bible was probably printed in _____.

Archbishop Cranmer and Thomas Cromwell obtained a _____ for this Bible.

It was also obtained for the _____ Bible. Now there were two _____ Bibles.

This first officially licensed Bible in the English language was essentially _____ Bible.

Where on Earth Did the Bible Come From?

In 1538, some bishops required that the Bible be _____.

This let the literate parishioners _____ the Bible and the illiterate parishioners could _____.

The *Coverdale Bible* was so popular that parishioners were _____.

The *Great Bible* was actually _____ revision of _____ revision of _____.

In 1543 restrictions were place on _____, except for the _____ Bible.

Mary Tudor was a strong _____ who massacred many of the Protestants, including _____.

Coverdale and others fled to _____. There he met with _____, _____, and _____.

They produced _____. A nickname for this Bible was _____, because of Genesis 3:7.

This was the first time the Bible was divided into _____.

This popular Bible soon became the favorite Bible of _____.

The *Geneva Bible* was the Bible of _____, _____, _____, and _____.

In reaction to the *Geneva Bible*, a committee of _____ produced their own Bible for use in public worship in the Church of England; they called this _____. It became the authorized Bible in the Church of England.

This version displaced the use of _____ in public worship in the Church of England. It eventually went through twenty editions in its forty-two years as the official basis for the King James Version.

14

The King James Version of the Bible

When Elizabeth I died in 1603, she left England at the height of its political and cultural glory. Having defeated the Spanish Armada, England increased its trade around the world and established colonies in America. English literature was at its height as never before—or afterward.

It was the era of Shakespeare, Marlowe, Bacon, Spenser, Bunyan, and other poets, who "one might say they invented the English language."[1] On the religious side, Elizabeth had strengthened the separation from the Pope, following in Henry VIII's path. As previously mentioned, there were three Bibles in use, which undermined attempts to unify England politically and culturally. The Catholics had their *Bishop's Bible,* the Protestants had their *Geneva Bible,* and the Church of England used the *Great Bible* in its worship services.

In addition to Church of England population, there was a restless Catholic minority and an emerging number of more extreme Calvinists separate from the established church, the Puritans.

---

1. Kerr, *Ancient Texts*, 109.

KING JAMES, THE MAN

In the midst of this politico-socio dynamic, arrived James VI, king of Scotland, son of Mary, Queen of Scots, and Lord Henry Darby.[2] His father was a great, great grandson of Henry VII of England, thus linked to the royal thrones of Scotland, Ireland, and England. His father was murdered, supposedly by his mother soon after James' birth. The family dynamics were a part of James' attitudes toward religion. He owed his throne to Queen Elizabeth, who had given the word to behead his mother.[3] With no heirs of her own, the throne fell to James.

His ascension to the throne marks the beginning of the House of Stuart.[4] James was a scholarly man with an inclination toward Protestant thinking. He was educated under George Buchanan, the greatest of the Scottish humanists and a supporter of the Reformation of the Church of Scotland. "James was bookish, uncertain, and somewhat shifty. He was effeminate in manners, a spendthrift, and intensely vain."[5] One modern biographer termed him "the wisest fool in Christendom."[6]

James I

2. See "Henry VIII of England."
3. Mathew, "James I."
4. See "James VI and I."
5. See "James VI and I."
6. See "James VI and I."

The King James Version of the Bible

However, James ruled the longest of any of his predecessors. He had been king of Scotland since he was one year old. He became King James I of England when he was thirty-nine years old. He had offended the Catholic population early on to the degree that several families plotted to assassinate him. They planted thirty-six barrels of gunpowder underneath the House of Lords where James was to address Parliament the next day, November 5, 1605. When the plot was discovered, because of their involvement in the plot, several Jesuit priests were executed. This act increased the general British anti-Catholic sentiment. Even two hundred years after, the English still celebrate "Guy Fawkes Day" to remember the deed. Because the Plague was rampantly killing thousands (thirty thousand) in London, a conference of leading churchmen was held at Hampton Court, a good distance from London. After the conference at Hampton Court in January 1604, where Catholics, Puritans, and Church of England representatives met with the king, one Puritan leader, John Reynolds, president of Corpus Christi College, Oxford, suggested that "there might be a new translation of the Bible because those used previously were corrupt." His suggestion was endorsed by Bishop Bancroft of London.

King James was excited about this idea. Bookish, literary James "would take more delight in shepherding a Bible translation than he would in building a palace, and certainly whose classical education aroused in him literary ambitions rarely found in princes but which also tended to make him a pedant [that, is a pseudointellectual]."[7] The king himself took a leading part in organizing the work of translation.[8] James, at thirty seven, was "a young old man who sputtered when he spoke because his tongue was too large for his mouth." However, Megan Mondi states that "his speeches reveal that he was an enlightened monarch who for the most part constructed his speeches carefully."[9] A condition existed in the motion for a new translation, however, that there be no marginal notes, except to explain the origin of particular words.

7. Mathew, "James I."
8. Bruce, *English Bible*, 97.
9. Mathew, "James I."

Thus, in a state of surprise bordering on shock, with an otherwise inefficient king spurring on the churchmen, the greatest of all English Bible translations began.

As an aside note, many Baptists and conservative evangelicals in America have held to the belief that the King James Version of the Bible is the only, true, divinely inspired translation of the Bible. Yet, King James, for all his excitement for the new Bible translation, was opposed to the concept of "freedom of religion" and "freedom of conscience." In 1612, one year after the publication of the new Bible, Thomas Helwys, one of the first Baptist preachers, wrote a pamphlet entitled, "*A Short Description of the Mistery of Iniquity*," in which he declared that, "The King is a mortall man, not God, therefore hath no power over ye immortal soules of his subjects to make laws and ordinances for them and to set spirituall Lords over them."[10]

This, plus another tract in stronger language, brought him imprisonment in New Gate Prison in 1612, by order of King James I. Little was heard of Helwys after release from prison, except that it is known he died prior to 1616.

The Learned Men, Translators

10. Torbet, *History of the Baptists*, 67; Childers, *Way Home*, 3.

THE LEARNED MEN

James ordered in February 1604 that the work "be done by the best learned in both Universities, after them to be reviewed by the Bishops and the chief learned of the Church; from them to be presented to the Privy-Council and lastly to be ratified by his Royal Authority; and so this whole Church to be bound unto it, and none other."[11]

The Dean of Westminster and the *Regius* Professors of Hebrew at both Oxford and Cambridge were asked to name one person competent for this task. By July 22, 1604, the king could write Bancroft that he had fifty-four men for the work. There were about fifty in all on the various lists, but only forty-seven on any one list. They represented the most able Bible scholarship of their time. The forty-seven men included most of the leading biblical scholars in England. They represented Catholic, Church of England, and Puritan groups.

One must remember that at this time the Puritans were still within the Church of England and had not yet separated from it, although, this would occur eventually. They received very little in the way of financial consideration during their work (neither king nor Parliament had much money to spare).[12]

The group divided into six companies. Each company had a specific part of the Bible to translate. Each company had as its leader the respective *Regius* Professors of Greek and Hebrew for Cambridge and Oxford, and the Dean of Westminster and the Dean of Chester. The work was divided among them as follows.[13]

1. *Genesis through 2 Kings* (Westminster company): Dr. Lancelot Andrews, Dr. John Overall, Dr. Hadrian Saravia, Dr. Richard Clarke, Dr. John Laifeld, Dr. Robert Tighe, Francis Burleigh, Geoffrey King, Richard Thompson, and Dr. William Bedwell.

2. *First Chronicles through Ecclesiastes* (Cambridge company): Edward Lively, Dr. John Richardson, Dr. Lawrence

---

11. Kerr, *Ancient Texts*, 114.
12. Bruce, *English Bible*, 98.
13. Bruce, *English Bible*, 114.

Chaderton, Francis Dillingham, Dr. Roger Andrews, Thomas Harrison, Dr. Robert Spaukling, and Dr. Andrew Bing.

3. *Isaiah through Malachi* (Oxford company): Dr. John Harding, Dr. John Reynolds, Dr. Thomas Holland, Dr. Richard Kilby, Dr. Miles Smith, Dr. Richard Brett, and Daniel Fairclouth.

4. *The Apocrypha* (Cambridge company): Dr. John Duport, Dr. William Brainthwaite, Dr. Jeremiah Radcliff, Dr. Samuel Ward, Dr. Andrew Downes, John Bois, Dr. Juon Ward, Dr. John Aglionby, Dr. Leonard Hutten, Dr. Thomas Bilson, and Dr. Richard Bancroft.

5. *The four Gospels, Acts, and Revelation* (Oxford company): Dr. Thomas Ravis, Dr. George Abbot, Dr. Richard Edes, Dr. Giles Tomson, Sir Henry Savile, Dr. John Peryn, Dr. Ralph Ravens, and Dr. John Harmar.

6. *Romans through Jude* (Westminster company): Dr. William Barlow, Dr. John Spencer, Dr. Roger Fenton, Dr. Ralph Hutchinson, William Dakins, Michael Rabber, Thomas Sanderson.

When the panels had completed their task, the draft translation of the whole Bible was reviewed by a smaller group of twelve men, two from each panel, and then the work was sent to the printer. Miles Smith, canon of Hereford (later to be bishop of Gloucester), and Thomas Bilson, bishop of Winchester, saw it through to the press.

The rules which guided them in their work were drawn up by James himself. They were:

1. The bishops' Bible was to serve as the basis for the new translation.

2. The names of Bible characters were to correspond as closely as possible to names in common use, but it did not attempt to maintain conformity between Old Testament and New Testament names.

3. The old ecclesiastical terms were to be kept—i.e., priest, penance.

4. Retain the existing chapter and verse divisions.
5. Chapter headings were to be supplied at the beginning of each chapter.

It is not often that a committee produces a monumental work of literature as did this team of scholars. Their translation is still read and loved and admired after nearly four hundred years.

The King James Version of the Bible

The King James Bible came about partly because forceful men thought they could use the project to further their private aims. Among the *Catholic representatives* at the Hampton Court meeting were: William Barlow, John Overall, Thomas Bilson, Richard Eves, and Lancelot Andrews. They were all good churchmen who courted James' favor, yet got along well with Rainolds and the Puritans.

Since the project began in early 1604, nearly three years went into preparatory work, two years and nine months went into actual translating, and another nine months preparing the final manuscript for the press. It came out in 1611 from the presses of Robert Barker, the king's printer.[14] The title of the Bible read:

> *The Holy Bible, conteyning the Old Testament and the New; Newly translated out of the Original Tongues: & with the former Translations diligently compared and reuised, by his Majesties speciall Commandment. Appointed to be read in Churches.*

The first edition contained some fifteen hundred pages. Eighteen pages were added in the front of the Bible, which included a dedication to King James. The rest of the introductory items were devotional or study aids: an almanac calendar listing all the holy days, morning and evening Scripture readings, a condensed almanac for thirty-nine years, a table "to find Easter forever," several lists of Scripture readings, and a chart of the books of the Bible, including the Apocrypha, with numbers or chapters in each.[15]

---

14. Kerr, *Ancient Texts*, 125.
15. Kerr, *Ancient Texts*, 126.

Words which were necessary for their sense in English, but were not in the original language, were printed in italics.

The first press run was twenty thousand copies. Because of the quantity, two presses were used, but the printing technology of the time would not permit "identical" printing. This led to discrepancies between the volumes printed on separate presses. The biggest discrepancy occurred in Ruth 3:15. One copy reads, "he measured six *measures* of barley and laid it on her, and he [Boaz] went into the city." The copy printed on the other press read, "and she [Ruth] went into the city." Thus, these two initial copies of the Bible are known as the "He" Bible and the "She" Bible. The problem lay in the fact that the Hebrew subject personal pronoun does not indicate gender. The translator has to look at the context of the phrase and draw the best conclusion.

The *King James Version* of the Bible has been revised many times to correct mistakes. In 1629 and 1638 corrections were made, but with each revision, more errors crept in. One printing in 1631 printed one of the Ten Commandments as, "Thou shalt commit adultery" (Exod 20:14). This came to be called "*The Wicked Bible*."[16] No one reads the *King James Version* in its original form.

Responses to the King James Version

Miles Smith wrote in the introduction to the *King James Version* of the Bible the anticipated criticisms of the new publication.[17]

> *Man mens mouthes haue bene open a good while (and yet are not stopped) with speeches about the Translation so long in hand . . .. And aske what may be the reason, what necessite of the employment.*

Criticism of the version was severe, as expected, and led to several immediate revisions. The revision of 1629 omitted the Apocrypha. The most extensive revisions were made by Thomas Paris at Cambridge in 1762 and by Benjamin Blayney at Oxford in

---

16. Kerr, *Ancient Texts*, 130.
17. Wikgren, "English Bible," 93.

The King James Version of the Bible

1769. This latter became the standard form for all newer revision. After this, few revisions were made.

With gradual improvement of the version, the opposition against it died down to a great extent. Officially, it replaced the *Bishops' Bible*, and after fifty years or so, it replaced the *Geneva Bible*, in popular use.[18] The bottom line is that the *King James Bible* remained the Bible of the English-speaking Protestants for two and a half centuries more and exerted a wide influence not only on religion, but on the development of the English language.

The Need for an English Language Catholic Bible

The focus of this study has been the development of Hebrew and Christian writings that have developed into the Bible used by the majority of English-speaking Protestants. It would be remiss not to mention that English-speaking Catholics shared a similar history in the development of the *Douay-Rheims Bible*. This is a history worthy of study equal to this. Unfortunately, this author realizes that he does not have the documents nor the knowledge to adequately undertake such a study. However, a glimpse of the history of the Douay-Rheims Bible is in order.

Because of persecution of Catholics by Elizabeth, some English Catholics fled to Douay, France where they established a Catholic college that was later moved to Rheims. The Catholic English translation was begun in Rheims in 1578 by Gregory Martin, an Oxford scholar and lecturer in Hebrew and the Bible. The New Testament was issued in 1582. Because of a lack of funds, the Old Testament was delayed until 1609–1610, by which time the college had returned to Douay.[19] In 1545, the Council of Trent laid down that a translation of the Bible should be based on the Latin Vulgate, rather than Hebrew and Greek translations. The Douay, or Douai, translation prefers the traditional ecclesiastical terms, derived from Latin, even if they were "out of touch" with the current

---

18. Wikgren, "English Bible," 95.
19. Huber, *Bible through the Ages*, 315. Also Bruce, *English Bible*, 114–15.

vernacular.[20] The Douay version seemed out of touch with the English language, as opposed to Tyndale and the "Learned Men." But one must remember that the Douay-Rheims version represents the losing side in the English Reformation conflict.[21] After 1610, from time to time, the Douai-Rheims translation received some slight revisions, but the most radical revision which has influenced all subsequent revisions was by Bishop Richard Challoner in 1738, with five more revisions in 1749 and 1772, of both the Old Testament and the New Testament. This was an attempt to make the Douay-Rheims version more readable to the Catholic population. One side note is that some of the translation appears more as interpretation than translation. The Douay-Rheims Bible was authorized for use by the English-speaking Roman Catholics of America in 1810. However, some of the marginal notes included in the early nineteenth century were "sufficiently forthright in their anti-Protestant vigor to cause considerable embarrassment to the Roman Catholic Bishops of Ireland during the Catholic Emancipation campaign."[22]

The conclusion of the matter is that both conflicting sides of the English Catholic-Protestant conflict have their version of God's written word to the point of being able to form conversation and eventual communion between themselves.

---

20. Bruce, *English Bible*, 117.
21. Bruce, *English Bible*, 120.
22. Bruce, *English Bible*, 126.

The King James Version of the Bible

CHAPTER 14 STUDY GUIDE

Some of the accomplishments of Queen Elizabeth were:

_____

_____

_____

_____

_____

It was the era of _____, _____, _____, and _____.

Elizabeth was the daughter of _____ and the sister of _____.

The three Bibles in use at this time were:

_____

_____

_____

The Protestants read _____ and the Catholics read _____. The Church of England used the _____.

The _____ was the Bible of the pilgrims and the first Bible in America.

The more extreme Calvinists in the Church of England were called the _____.

The new king was _____ of Scotland, son of _____, and grandson of _____.

James' ascension to the throne was the beginning of the House of _____.

One modern biographer termed him "_____."

James had been king of Scotland since he was _____.

And he became king of England when he was _____.

Where on Earth Did the Bible Come From?

- On November 5, 1605, a plot to blow up Parliament and the king was called _____.
- A terrible condition in London during this time, killing thousands of people, was _____.
- In a conference at Hampton Court, _____ suggested there was need for a new Bible. He was later called "the Father of the King James Bible."
- James sputtering speech problem was because _____.
- In spite of James' excitement about the new Bible, he imprisoned _____ for advocating freedom of conscience.
- This man was one of the first Baptist preachers: _____
- The men selected to translate the Bible were called _____.
- The number of translators was _____. They were divided into _____ companies. The companies represented _____, _____, _____, and _____.
- Each company translated _____.
- The actual translation work took _____.
- The total project took _____.
- The book was dedicated to _____.
- The first press run was _____ copies.
- The King James Version of the Bible has been _____ many times.
- One printing in 1631 was called "The Wicked Bible" because it printed one of the Ten Commandments as _____.

The King James Version of the Bible

Because of _____, there were several immediate revisions.

The KJV officially replaced the _____.

It remained the Bible of the _____.

It was also the Bible of _____, _____, _____, and _____.

The King James Version of the Bible impacted not only _____, but also _____ and _____.

The _____ also needed an English language Bible. English Catholics were persecuted and driven to live in _____.

_____ saw the need for an English language Bible for Catholics.

He started a college in _____ and later moved it to _____.

Thus, the name of the Catholic English Bible is _____ _____.

The most significant revision of this Bible was done by _____ in _____.

This should permit both Protestant and Catholic English-Speaking groups to be able to _____ _____.

147

Bibliography

Anderson, G. W. *A Critical Introduction to the Old Testament*. London: Duckworth, 1959.
"Baptism in Early Christianity." https://en.wikipedia.org/wiki/Baptism_in_early_Christianity.
Barclay, William. *The Gospel of Matthew*. Philadelphia: Westminster, 1959.
———. *The Letters of James and Peter*. Philadelphia: Westminster, 1956.
———. *The Letters to the Philippians, Colossians, and Thessalonians*. Philadelphia: Westminster, 1956.
Barrett, C. K. *The New Testament Background*. New York: Harper, 1961.
Beecher, Willis J. *The Prophets and the Promise*. Grand Rapids: Baker, 1963.
Bettenson, Henry. *Documents of the Christian Church*. London: Oxford University Press, 2011.
Bow, J. G. *What Baptists Believe and Why they Believe It*. Nashville: The Sunday School Board of the Southern Baptist Convention, 1958.
Bright, John. *A History of Israel*. Philadelphia: Westminster, 2000.
Browne, Lewis. *The Wisdom of Israel*. New York: Random House, 1945.
Bruce, F. F. "The Canon of the New Testament." http://www.bible-researcher.com/bruce1.html. 1961.
———. *The English Bible*. New York: Oxford University Press,
Butterfield, Hubert. *Christianity and History*. New York: Scribner's, 1960.
Buttrick, George Arthur, et al., eds. *The Interpreter's Bible*. 12 vols. Nashville: Abingdon, 1951–57.
Cadbury, C. J. "The New Testament and Early Christian Literature." In *The Interpreter's Bible: General Articles on the New Testament, Matthew, Mark*, edited by George Arthur Buttrick et al., 7:32–42. New York: Abingdon, 1951.
Cadbury, Henry J. *The Making of Luke–Acts*. London: SPCK, 1961.
Campbell, Joseph. *The Masks of God: Oriental Mythology*. New York: Viking, 1991.
Campbell-Reed, Eileene. *Being Baptist*. Macon, GA: Smyth & Helwys, 1998.
"Canon." www.biblestudytools.com/dictionary/canon/.

Bibliography

Childers, James Saxton. *A Way Home: The Baptists Tell Their Story.* New York: Holt, Rinehart & Winston, 1964.

Clark, Kenneth W. "The Transmission of the New Testament." In *The Interpreter's Bible: James, Peter, John, Jude, Revelation, General Articles*, edited by George Arthur Buttrick et al., 12:617–27. New York: Abingdon, 1957.

Cohen, Mortimer J. *Pathways through the Bible.* Philadelphia: Jewish Publication Society of America, 1959.

Colwell, Ernest C. "Text and Ancient Versions of the New Testament." In *The Interpreter's Bible: General and Old Testament Articles, Genesis, Exodus*, edited by George Arthur Buttrick et al., 1:72–83. Nashville: Abingdon, 1952.

Conzelmann, Hans. *The Theology of Saint Luke.* London: Faber & Faber, 1961.

Cook, Henry. *What Baptists Stand For.* London: Kingsgate, 1961.

Cranfield, C. E. B. *I & II Peter and Jude.* London: SCM, 1955.

Cross, Frank Moore. *The Dead Sea Scrolls.* Washington, DC: Biblical Archaeology Society, 2007.

Cullman, Oscar. *Peter: Disciple, Apostle, Martyr.* Cleveland: Meridian, 1953.

DeWeese, Charles W. *Freedom: The Key to the Baptist Genius.* Brentwood, TN: Baptist History and Heritage Society, 2006.

Dodd, C. H. *The Interpretation of the Fourth Gospel.* Cambridge: Cambridge University Press, 1965.

———. *Johannine Epistles.* New York: Harper, 1946.

Easton, Matthew George. "Entry for Canon." www.biblestudytools.com/dictionary/canon/.

Elliott, Ralph H. *The Message of Genesis.* Nashville: Broadman, 1964.

"English Bible History." https://www.greatsite.com/timeline-english-bible-history/.

Fosbroke, Hughell E.W. "The Prophetic Literature." In *The Interpreter's Bible: General and Old Testament Articles, Genesis, Exodus*, edited by George Arthur Buttrick et al., 1:201–11. New York: Abingdon, 1952.

Francisco, Clyde. *Introducing the Old Testament.* Nashville: Broadman, 1950.

Friedman, Richard Elliott. *Who Wrote the Bible?* New York: Simon & Schuster, 1997.

Gaer, Joseph. *How the Great Religions Began.* New York: Dodd, Mead, 1956.

"The Geneva: Bible of the Pilgrims & Puritans." https://greatsite.com/ancient-rare-bible-leaves/geneva-leaf.html.

Goodspeed, Edgar J. "The Canon of the New Testament." In *The Interpreter's Bible: General and Old Testament Articles, Genesis, Exodus*, edited by George Arthur Buttrick et al., 1:63–71. Nashville: Abingdon, 1952.

———. *How Came the Bible?* New York: Abingdon, 1981.

Grant, Robert M. "History of the Interpretation of the Bible." In *The Interpreter's Bible: General and Old Testament Articles, Genesis, Exodus*, edited by George Arthur Buttrick et al., 1:106–14. New York: Abingdon, 1952.

Graves, Dan. "John Rogers, 1st of Many Martyrs." https://www.christianity.com/church/church-history/timeline/1501-1600/john-rogers-1st-of-many-martyrs-11629985.html.

BIBLIOGRAPHY

Guillaumont, Antoine. *The Gospel According to Thomas.* Leiden: Brill, 2001.
"Hasmonean Dynasty." https://en.wikipedia.org/wiki/Hasmonean_dynasty.
Hatch, William H. B. "The Life of Paul." In *The Interpreter's Bible: James, Peter, John, Jude, Revelation, General Articles,* edited by George Arthur Buttrick et al., 12:187-99. Nashville: Abingdon, 1956.
Hayes, Brooks. "On My Baptist Faith." In *A Way Home,* by James Saxton Childers, 16. New York: Holt, Winston & Reinhart, 1964.
"Henry VIII of England." https://en.wikipedia.org/wiki/Henry_VIII_of_England.
Herklots, H. G. G. *How Our Bible Came To Us.* New York: Oxford University Press, 1957
Hester, H. I. *The Heart of Hebrew History.* Liberty, MO: Jewel, 1949.
Hock, Ronald F. *The Infancy Gospels of James and Thomas.* Santa Rosa, CA: Polebridge, 1995.
Huber, Robert V., ed. *The Bible through the Ages: Examination of the Land, Laws, Traditions, and Customs of the Ancient Near East.* Pleasantville, NY: Reader's Digest Association, 1996.
Hull, William E. *The Meaning of the Baptist Experience.* The New Baptist Covenant Edition. Atlanta: Baptist History and Heritage Society, 2008.
Hunter, Archibald M. "The First Epistle of Peter." In *The Interpreter's Bible: Philippians, Colossians, Thessalonians, Pastoral Epistles, Philemon, Hebrews,* edited by George Arthur Buttrick et al., 11:75-159. New York: Abingdon, 1955.
Irwin, William A. "The Wisdom Literature." In *The Interpreter's Bible: General and Old Testament Articles, Genesis, Exodus,* edited by George Arthur Buttrick et al., 1:212-19. New York: Abingdon, 1952.
"James VI and I." https://en.wikipedia.org/wiki/James_VI_and_I.
Jeffery, Arthur. "The Formation and Transmission of the Old Testament." In *The Interpreter's Bible: General and Old Testament Articles, Genesis, Exodus,* edited by George Arthur Buttrick et al., 1:32-62. New York: Abingdon, 1952.
"Jerome." https://en.wikipedia.org/wiki/Jerome.
"John Colet." Greatsite.com/timeline-english-bible-history/john-colet.
Kasser, Rudolph, et al. *The Gospel of Judas.* Washington, DC: The National Geographic Society, 2006.
Kerr, John Stevens. *Ancient Texts Alive Today.* Edited by Charles Houser. New York: American Bible Society, 1999.
Koch, Klaus. *The Growth of the Biblical Tradition.* New York: Scribner's, 1969.
Köhler, Ludwig. *Hebrew Man, How He Looked, Lived, and Thought.* New York: Abingdon, 1956.
Krosney, Herbert. *The Lost Gospel: The Quest for the Gospel of Judas Iscariot.* Washington, DC: The National Geographic Society, 2006.
Lawson, James Gilcrest. *The Best Loved Religious Poems: Gleaned from Many Sources.* New York: Revell, 1963.

Bibliography

Levine, Amy-Jill. *The Old Testament*. Chantilly, VA: The Teaching Company, 2001.
Lewis, C. S. *Reflections on the Psalms*. New York: Harcourt, Brace & World, 1958.
Lightfoot, Neil R. *How We Got the Bible*. New York: MJF Books, 2003.
Lindsell, Howard. *The Harper Study Bible: Revised Standard Version*. New York: Harper & Row, 1962.
Lissner, Ivar. *Man, God, and Magic*. New York: Putnam's, 1961.
Lumpkin, W. L. *Baptist Confessions of Faith*. Chicago: Judson, 1959.
Manson, William. *The Gospel of Luke*. London: Hodder & Stoughton, 1963.
Mathew, David. "James I." https://www.britannica.com/biography/James-I-king-of-England-and-Scotland.
Moody, Dale. *Christ and the Church: An Exposition of Ephesians*. Grand Rapids: Eerdmans, 1963.
"Native Tribes of Britain." https://www.bbc.co.uk/history/ancient/british_prehistory/iron_01.shtml.
Norwood, Frederick A. *The Development of Modern Christianity Since 1500*. New York: Abingdon, 1956.
Noss, John B. *Man's Religions*. New York: Macmillan, 1980.
Pagels, Elaine. *Beyond Belief: The Secret Gospel of Thomas*. New York: Random House, 2005.
Paine, Gustavus S. *The Learned Men*. New York: Crowell, 1959.
"Parthian Empire." https://en.wikipedia.org/wiki/Parthian_Empire.
Perry, Alfred M. "The Growth of the Gospels." In *The Interpreter's Bible: General Articles on the New Testament, Matthew, Mark*, edited by George Arthur Buttrick et al., 7:60–74. Nashville: Abingdon, 1951.
Peters, Ellis. *Brother Cadfael Chronicles*. New York: Mysterious Press, 1994.
Pollard, Alfred W. *Records of the English Bible*. Oxford: Frowde, 1911.
Richardson, Alan. *Genesis 1–11*. London: SCM, 1953.
Rimmer, Sandra. "Maps of Britain and Ireland's Ancient Tribes, Kingdoms and DNA." http://www.abroadintheyard.com/maps-britain-ireland-ancient-tribes.
Robertson, A. T. *Paul and the Intellectuals*. Nashville: Broadman, 1959.
Robinson, James M., ed. *The Nag Hamadi Library*. New York: Harper & Row, 1977.
Schürer, Emil. *A History of the Jewish People in the Time of Jesus*. New York: Schoken, 1961.
Scott, Ernest F. "The History of the Early Church, Part 1: The Beginnings." In *The Interpreter's Bible: General Articles on the New Testament, Matthew, Mark*, edited by George Arthur Buttrick et al., 7:176–86. Nashville: Abingdon, 1951.
"Seleucid Empire." https://en.wikipedia.org/wiki/Seleucid_Empire.
Serfes, Demetrios. "Holy Scripture in the Orthodox Church: 'The Bible.'" *Orthodox Spirituality* (blog), August 20, 2000. http://www.serfes.org/orthodox/scripturesinthechurch.htm.

BIBLIOGRAPHY

Shurden, Walter B. *The Baptist Identity: Four Fragile Freedoms*. Macon: Smyth & Helwys, 1993.
Smith, T. C. *How We Got Our Bible*. Macon: Smyth & Helwys, 1995.
Stagg, Frank. *The Book of Acts*. Nashville: Broadman, 1955.
Stealy, Syndor L. *A Baptist Treasury*. New York: Crowell, 1958.
Torbet, Robert. *A History of the Baptists*. Philadelphia: Judson, 1950.
Tribble, H. W., et al. *Old Testament Biographies*. Nashville: Broadman, 1935.
Votaw, Clyde Weber. "Martyrs for the English Bible." *The Biblical World* 52 (November 1918) 296–99. https://www.jstor.org/stable/3135994?seq=1#page_scan_tab_contents.
"Vulgate." https://en.wikipedia.org/wiki/Vulgate
Walker, Williston, et al. *A History of the Christian Church*. New York: Scribner's, 1985.
Wallace, Daniel B. "From Wycliffe to King James (the Period of Challenge)." https://bible.org/seriespage/1-wycliffe-king-james-period-challenge.
Weiss, Johannes. *Earliest Christianity: A History of the Period A. D. 30–150*. 2 vols. New York: Smith, 1984.
"What Are the Different Theories of Biblical Inspiration?" https://www.gotquestions.org/inspiration-theories.html.
"When Were the Bible Books Written?" https://www.gty.org/library/questions/qa176/when-were-the-bible-books-written.
"Who Were the King James Version Translators?" https://www.jesus-is-lord.com/transtoc.htm.
Wikgren, Allen. "The English Bible." In *The Interpreter's Bible: General and Old Testament Articles, Genesis, Exodus*, edited by George Arthur Buttrick et al., 1:84–105. New York: Abingdon, 1957.
Williams, Paul O. "The Men Who Risked All to Translate the Bible." *The Christian Science Monitor*, July 26, 2001. https://www.csmonitor.com/2001/0726/p21s1.html.
"Wycliffe 1731 New Testament Reproduction." http://greatsite.com/facsimile-reproductions/wycliffe-1731-detail3.html.

Scripture Index

OLD TESTAMENT

Genesis
1:1—11	16
1:1—2:3	17
2:4—25	17
3:7	131
3:34	17
6:1—8	17
6:19	17
7:2	17
12:6	16
12:10–20	17
13:7	18
15:4	17
16:4–14	17
16:19	17
17:16	17
17:17–19	17
18:12–13	17
18:10	17
20:1–18	17
21:6	17
21:9–21	17
21:34	18
26:1	18
36:31	18
40:15	17

Exodus
20:14	132, 142

Joshua
1–7	36
8–22	36
23–24	36

Judges
5	22

Ruth
3:15	142

I Samuel
10:10	37

2 Samuel
24:11	34, 37

I Chronicles
3:17–24	24

I Kings
3:6–9	41

2 Kings
22–23	25

Psalms
4:1–2	40
23	40
40:1–3	40
91:5	132
119:161	132

Scripture Index

Ezekiel
14:14	41
14:20	41

Daniel
2:4—7:28	16

Ezra
4:8—6:18	16
7:27—9:15	16, 28,
18—16	28

Nehemiah
12:10	10, 11, 12, 22, 28

Isaiah
1:1	37

Amos
8:4-6	38

Micah
2:1—2	38
2:12	38, 39
21:38	38

NEW TESTAMENT

Matthew
13:3-5	106
6:3—13	106
19:21	91

Mark
14:51	47, 52
16:9-20	54

Luke
1:3	62
1:1-4	13, 47, 53, 75
2:17-19	43
2:19	54
6:17	54
24:6	132
28:30—31	63

John
1:1- 5	3, 55
16:13	3
19:20	55
20:30-31	76
20:30	3, 47, 55
21:24-25	13, 47, 48, 76

Acts
12:12	52
28:30-31	

Romans
1:20	18

I Corinthians
5:9	61
13	62
15:51-58	43
16:21	61

Galatians
1:6	61

Colossians
4:18	60

I Thessalonians
1:1	60

2 Thessalonians
3:17	61

2 Timothy
3:16-17	61

Hebrews
1:1-2	1, 42, 62
4:12—13	63
4:14	63, 66,
10:23	66

I Peter
5:12	65

SCRIPTURE INDEX

OTHER CHRISTIAN WRITINGS *

The Acts of Andrew	73, 75
The Acts of John	73, 75
The Acts of Paul	73, 75
Apology of Justin	67
The Didache	72, 73, 75
The Epis of Barnabas	63, 72, 73, 75
The Epis of Apostles	67
The Epis of Polycarp	63
First, Second Clement	50, 63, 75
The Gospel of Peter	67, 73, 75
Gospel According Hebrews	72, 82
Gospel of Thomas	73, 75
Gospel of Matthias	73, 75
Interp of Papias	67
The Preach of Peter	67
The Shep of Hermas	63, 67, 72, 73

The Apocrypha

Tobit	83
Judith	83
Wisdom	83
Baruch	83
Letter of Jeremiah	83
Ecclesiasticus	83
1 & 2 Maccabees	83
Prayer of Manassas	83
Laodeceans	83

www.ingramcontent.com/pod-product-compliance
Lightning Source LLC
Chambersburg PA
CBHW050816160426
43192CB00010B/1787